STUNTS:

THE HOW TO HANDBOOK

SECRETS FROM AN AWARD WINNING HOLLYWOOD STUNT WOMAN

ANGELA MERYL

EDITED BY
MICHAEL ANDRE ADAMS

XXXXXX Publications

2011

www.angelameryl.com

Copyright 2011 by Angela Meryl

P.O. Box 571544

Tarzana, CA. 91356

www.angelameryl.com

Library of Congress Control Number: 2012908022

Leximeryl, Tarzana CA

ISBN-10: 0615579094

ISBN-13: 978-0615579092

Printed in the United States of America

Cover Photo Credit: Shawn Barber

Table of Contents

Introduction

It was April 21, 2010, a day I will always remember. On that chilly Chicago morning the blustery winds howled fiercely. Still I managed to stand motionless, five stories above the ground with my feet firmly planted on the very edge of the roof at Harpo Studios.

Trying my best to think warm, I waited anxiously for the cue to strategically fall to the ground. Desperately I fought with all my might against the relentless gusts of wind doing everything possible to push me over the edge.

Photo Credit:
Russell Baer

A safe landing meant going live, one-on-one, with the legendary Oprah Winfrey. Imagine that: The queen of daytime television and me – stuntwoman Angela Meryl. The thrill of it all still gives me butterflies in my stomach.

The lyrics from a song by rapper Eminem, ran nonstop through my mind that day: "You only get one shot; do not miss your chance to blow."

And there I was, standing high in the sky with just one shot to impress the woman who redefined talk TV.

With 14 years of calculated and other times flat out daredevil career success under my belt, and another two days of practice jumping in Los Angeles, prior to a full crew rehearsal in Chicago, I was ready, as in 110-percent ready to take the fall. Still, every thought about my state of being in that moment had a chilling effect on me. It was like a state of euphoria based on where I came from and what the future might hold.

Now I can understand why people who don't do stunts drink, smoke, do drugs or whatever else to get high, which is really nothing more than an altered state of reality. For me, the high that day was the chance jump down and sit with a living legend to explain before the eyes of millions of viewers around the world – how and why my choice to make a career of doing stunts IS my dream job.

But on that day my head was spinning and not just because of my own thoughts either. There were directions coming at me from left to right. Show producers, the stunt coordinator and the technical crew all had a laundry list of imperative instructions for me to follow. Things like what to do, when and how each should be done where to land, what to do when I get up, where to go so I could look my best for Oprah were in addition to what I needed to do as a stunt professional to in order to execute a safe fall. It was a helluva lot to focus on at a very exciting time in my career. The energy was so intense that day that on several occasions I had to pinch myself to be sure I wasn't at home in a daze, staring at my vision board.

How it All Happened

On the morning of April Fool's Day 2010, my friend and publicist called to tell me about a conversation he had with a producer from Harpo Productions in Chicago.

"Angela," he said, "I need you to do a preliminary interview with a producer from 'The Oprah Winfrey Show.'"

They're doing a show on dream jobs and have an interest in your life and work as a stuntwoman."

" 'The Oprah Winfrey Show'! Yeah right, April's Fool!" I said to him.

Because we're old friends, we both laughed out loud! Afterwards, he put forth his best efforts to persuade me that it wasn't a joke. To prove the point he dialed the producer's telephone number, connecting us on a three-way call. Although there was no answer, the outgoing message identified the name of the person he claimed to had just spoken with as a producer for *"The Oprah Winfrey Show."*

Absolutely stunned from what I heard, the sound of my whimpers accompanied by tears of joy began to flow. To hear my publicist tell the story today, it was as dramatic as a funeral scene in a comedy movie. But to me it was more like Halle Berry receiving the Oscar Award: It was an emotional recount of the many years I've spent training, watching, listening and learning to be better than the best I can be. To meet the requirements of every job, I give 110 percent! Through it all, rarely, if ever have I stopped to really focus on the acknowledgements from others who applaud my work.

Having had my share of experiences with people who are less than sincere or have hidden agendas, I tend to take compliments with caution. But to even be considered as a guest on a show hosted by a woman the world knows on a first name basis by a name synonymous with honesty and sincerity, was the pat on the back that further validates my career as a stuntwoman and says that what I do really does matter.

The very next day, my publicist had arranged for me to speak with the producer, Colleen. She made it clear from the very start of the conversation that they were interviewing lots of people from all over the world for a show about dream jobs. They were on a hunt for interesting people who do spectacular things in their respective careers and wanted to know more about my job, which sounded quite exciting based on all that my publicist had already told them. Colleen asked questions such as how I got into the stunt business, which of the most daring stunts were my favorites, what celebrities I liked best to double and what drastic challenges had I gone through to perform.

She wanted and needed a taste of the good, the bad and the ugly. While tracing back over the years of my career my face lit up like a Christmas tree on several occasions. I thought about the many action-packed stunts I've performed over the years, escaping major injury or worse, meaning I had cheated death a time or two.

But for Colleen, it was the mention of doubling Halle Berry, Beyoncé, Vivica A. Fox, Vanessa Williams and Gabriel Union – my "Fab Five" leading ladies – that struck her fancy. I guess that goes to say that anyone can be star-struck, including a producer from "*The Oprah Winfrey Show.*" Before exiting the call, Colleen said, "Oprah thought it would be kind of cool if you jumped off the roof of the building."

The split second thought to myself was, "Well I sure hope she's not in the Sears Tower!" I then paused, took a breath and asked, "How tall is the building?" Colleen wasn't sure. But she said she would get back to me with measurements.

Seconds after I hung up the phone, I knew without a doubt that I wanted to be on "*The Oprah Winfrey Show.*" And I wanted this more than anything I had ever wanted in my life. Come on! Oprah and me on television! That was a dream job in itself!

Over and over I attempted to convince myself by saying out loud: "I've got a shot at this." That quickly turned into. "I'm getting this." Over and over, louder and louder as though it were a chant, I spoke it to the universe, "I'm getting this!"

To help bring it to fruition, I placed a photograph of Oprah on a very special goal board that hangs in my office above the desk – one that I found online at myvisiongoals.com. Framed in a beautiful gold-leaf wood, it houses pictures and phrases of the people, places and things I decide to bring into my life. Because it's made of cork, I can easily pin things on it that can be removed once achieved. Along with the picture of Oprah on my goal board, I added the words "My Dream Job Show."

Later that same day, Colleen called to tell me the building is four stories tall. She promised to act with urgency and also send pictures via e-mail.

It was a quick call that concluded with Colleen telling me she'd get back to me if there was any further interest. In other words, "Don't call us; we'll call you!"

But that didn't scare me. Instead, I affirmed once more, saying, "I have a shot at this. I'm getting this."

Then, I let it go. Three weeks later, Colleen's call caught me by total surprise. Somehow in my mind I thought it would have been months later before I had heard back from her.

She called to tell me they were narrowing their choices and had a few more questions to ask.

"*YES*," I said silently to myself while clinching my fist as though I were Tiger Woods after htting a hole-in-one! During the next 20-minutes of the call, Colleen must have asked a thousand detailed questions about my experiences of performing stunts. She called back about four more times that day. Each time she wanted more details of the stunts I had performed.

Obviously, she was in need of the wow factor. So I delivered. I told her about the good, the bad and the ugly side of this business. At the end of every call she would always pledge to talk with her boss and let me know something soon. In one subsequent call I'll never forget her saying, "We really love you here, Angela." The sound of such encouraging words was like sweet music to my ears, drawing me closer and closer to believing I would appear on the "*The Oprah Winfrey Show*."

My affirmations seemed to be working. Early one Saturday morning – about 7:30 on the West coast – the phone rang. I was still in a deep sleep trying to recover from the weekly grind of balancing a stunt career with the joyful, never-ending activities of parenting my then 3-year-old daughter. It was Colleen, the producer from "*The Oprah Winfrey Show*." Without any hesitation, she said they wanted to book me for the show in Chicago. In practically the same breath she said they wanted me there in two days to perform a death-defying jump from the rooftop of Harpo Studios to demonstrate the love I have for my career as a stuntwoman.

"*Hell yeah*," I said to myself from cloud nine, after which I uttered, "Sure." – all calm and cool, to Colleen.

Seconds later, after ending the call, I hung up the phone and leaped out of bed to call my mom. "*Mommy, mommy, Oprah Winfrey wants to interview me.*" Just like I didn't believe my publicist at first, my mom didn't believe me either, which goes to prove the fruit never falls far from the tree.

Over and over my mom kept saying, "Stop joking." In between all the laughter, I told my mom I wanted her to accompany me to Chicago. Finally, she began to believe me. Between the calls from Colleen and to my mom, it was a Saturday morning I will always remember.

Preparation Meets Opportunity

It had been eight years since the last time I practiced high falls. Thank God I know people like Bob Yerkes, a former circus performer with a 100-foot tower and lots of airbags in his back yard. His home serves as a training ground for many stunt performers to practice fights, high and low-falls, air-rams, wire work, flips on trampolines and more. To a stunt person, a visit to Bob's is sort of like going to a playground, where you can hang out all day while perfecting your skills.

When I called to ask Bob if I could come over to practice he said, "Sure, come right over."

Immediately, I was on my way with friend and fellow stunt performer, Dakota Bown in tow. Dakota and Bob are friends from way back. She's known him a whole lot longer than I have. With lots of guidance from Dakota, my practice falls began from 10 feet, then to 12-feet, while landing on a thick, soft mat called a porta pit. From there I graduated to 15-, 20-, 25- and then 30-feet falls. It seemed as if the narrow little ladder I had to climb to position myself for the fall, rose to a 90-degree angle. The higher I climbed, the smaller the platform at the top became. And it was only about 10-inces wide and 12-inches long to start.

Before long, I had worked my way up to a 40-foot fall, which is about the same distance as the four-story building from which Oprah wanted me to jump. So that I'd have extra cushioning for the higher falls, Bob pulled out his heavy-duty airbag – the one with a fall rating of 50 feet. It reminds me of a big whoopee cushion in the sense that while completely embracing me, it lets out a little air in the process.

After two days of practicing at Bob's, I felt confident and absolutely sure that I could nail the landing on live TV, knowing my life and my career in stunts was depending on it. I was ready to fall for Oprah!

Off to Chicago

Two days following Colleen's call, a Lincoln Town Car pulled into the driveway of my Los Angeles home. If you live in Los Angeles, work in the entertainment industry and have the income to support it, a Town Car is the only way to get to and from LAX Airport. This time the ride was on Oprah.

The driver took the most direct and time-sensitive route to get there, traveling down the notorious Interstate 405, where traffic can be a nightmare. But that day everything was going my way. Even inside the airport, the cumbersome process of passing through security checkpoints seemed stressed-free on my way to meet Oprah. I took my full-size leather seat in first-class and ordered a glass of cranberry juice from a kind flight attendant. It was tough, but I managed to refrain from telling every passenger walking by that I was about to be interviewed by Oprah. Seriously, I sat there practically giggling like a schoolgirl. At the time the entire experience all seemed so surreal. Throughout the entire flight, I closed my eyes over and over again to envision the stunt I was about to perform. Each time my landing was perfect. That made me smile. But all of sudden, it hit me that this shy woman was about to be in the spotlight, smack dab in the eyes of millions of viewers.

I had no idea what questions the queen of daytime television might ask, which made me just a little bit nervous. But as quickly as those thoughts came to mind, I could suddenly see the smiling face of my daughter with her arms stretched open to give mommy a great big ole hug. In an instant, that and the fact that my own mom was flying in from Philadelphia to be with me, gave me the assurance I needed, which was far nicer than being bitch-slapped by a friend and told to snap out of it! Arriving in Chicago a few hours later, I realized that Team Oprah does things first-class all the way. In addition to the Town Car that got me to the airport, a driver was waiting for me at the airport in Chicago – holding a sign with my name in the baggage claim area. After he collected my luggage, we were off to the Omni Hotel on Michigan Avenue – in yet another Town Car, of course. After check-in, I discovered that the room Harpo reserved for me was a very comfortable suite. To celebrate it all – the suite, the show, the successful fall I was about to take – I ordered almost everything on the menu that appealed to me; Two flat breads (or pizzas, depending on the chef who's making them), salad, soup, even a piece of fish. But it was the Spence Farms white truffle popcorn that stole the show. It was so good that I asked for a container, so I could seal it up to keep it fresh for my enjoyment hroughout the two-night stay. All that excitement really helped to prepare me for what I was about to do. So, that night I slept like a baby.

The Rehearsal

By 11:30 the next morning, I was at Harpo Studios, where stunt coordinator Rick Le Fevour had me positioned four stories up in the air on a scissor lift for the practice fall. Up there, the eye tearing, ice-cold, gusty winds were far more intense than down on the ground below. The wind blew so hard that I had to constantly swipe the hair from my face just so I could see.

Speaking of the ground, I noticed a crowd assembling below on the street. I could see some of them pointing up at me. My guess is they were probably wondering what on earth Oprah was about to do now! Even traffic appeared to be slowing down to focus on the action. The excitement had me grinning from cheek to cheek, with butterflies in my stomach.

The stunt coordinator's plan was for me to fall from the scissor lift and land on the airbag four stories below. But, what if the wind blew me off course, and I totally overshot the airbag?

As that thought entered my mind, I reflected on former stunt colleague Sonja Davis, who died on the set of "*Vampire in Brooklyn*," starring Eddie Murphy and Angela Basset. Her grieving mother told the Los Angeles Times, "The airbag reacted like a huge balloon, causing Sonja to bounce, slam into the building and hit the ground."

Such a thought could scare anyone, including me for a few seconds. But then I looked back over my 14 years of expertise as a stuntwoman. I recalled a day I rappelled from a helicopter hovering about 10-stories in the sky and landed beautifully. I thought about the time I ran through a doorway while engulfed in flames. I walked away without a single burn to my body. Then there was a time when amidst the strong currents and grungy undertow of New York's Hudson River, I had to lie face down and play dead with ankle weights attached. Ferry after ferry passed by, creating swells in the water that made the stunt even more challenging. Again, after all of that I thought, surely I can fall four stories to the ground to meet Oprah. Right then, I imagined hearing Isaac Hayes singing my theme song: "That chick Angela is a bad mutha ... shut ya mouth!" And once again, I was good to go. All three practice jumps went off without a hitch. I hit the X in the center of the bag every time. Soon thereafter I was driven back to The Omni with more excitement in my mind and stomach.

My mom was now in Chicago, too. Having her fly in from Philadelphia to be with me was as exciting for me as it was for her. Unfortunately, living bicoastal means I don't get to see her as often, since she lives solely on the east coast.

Because it was mom's first time in Chicago, we decided to walk around the famous Magnificent Mile district. Window shopping, manicures and popcorn from world-renowned Garrett Popcorn Shop on Michigan Avenue – one of Oprah's "Favorite Things" – helped us pass the time that afternoon.

Once we returned to the hotel, we stayed there for the remainder of the day to prepare for our 6 o'clock pickup the next morning. There was one exception: I ran back out and around the corner from the hotel to Gino's East, for pizza.

It took 45-minutes to make the thick, deep-dish vegetarian pizza with chunks of tomatoes, peppers, mushrooms and onions. It must have weighed a ton. But every slice was finger-licking good. In fact, on a scale of 1-10, with 10 being the absolute best, it was a 10-plus.

Later that night – the eve of my long-awaited interview on "The Oprah Winfrey Show" – I thought about everything that had shaped my life and career to date. Having someone there to share it – someone as dear to me as my mom – meant more than I can ever fully express in words. That alone was a high point in my career.

Then came the 5 a.m. call from the hotel operator. With hair and makeup waiting for me on the set I only had to get up, washed, dressed and downstairs to the car. Along the way to the studio that Wednesday morning, I could hardly contain my joy. "What's that building," I asked the driver as he drove down Magnificent Mile. "*Wow, look at the great architecture*," I said out of nervous energy. All along I wanted so badly to stick my head out of the window and scream out to the top of my lungs: "*I'm going on Oprah today!*"

The Harpo Experience

When the 20-minute thrill ride ended, we were at Harpo Studios. The first thing I noticed was a line of people standing outside on the sidewalk. I'd say from about 50 to 100 people at least. My guess is they were probably waiting to see Oprah.

Well, OK. ...Oprah ... and me! Then the chauffeur got out and went to the door by himself. Seconds later he returned to the car to escort mom and me to the front entrance. As excited as we were, a sign that was impossible to ignore almost killed our joy. It stated that no cameras or phones were allowed beyond a certain point. And with Twitter being all the rage, I had planned on tweeting until the very second before I jumped.

With that option no longer at my fingertips, I decided to stop where I was and step back to get one quick tweet out, along with a note to my Facebook friends. It read: "I'm doing a stunt on "*Oprah*" today. Please watch."

When we arrived inside the studio Colleen, the producer who now felt like my friend, was waiting to greet me. It felt so good to finally meet face to face, especially after the many conversations I had had with her and Eileen, another Oprah staffer.

Eileen, whose name you haven't heard until now, came onto the scene after I was booked to perform the stunt. Her first call was to request a picture of me for the show. She specifically asked for a personal picture. Via e-mail, I included pictures alongside each of my "Fab-Five" list of leading ladies I had doubled. Throughout the day, Eileen e-mailed me six times. After that she seemed absolutely convinced she had the perfect picture. Throughout Harpo Studios, walls were decorated with pictures of the many celebrity guests who had appeared on "The Oprah Winfrey Show" over its 25-year run. While laughing to myself, and still somewhat serious, I wondered where Oprah might hang my picture. Awaiting in the green room was a beautiful summer fruit basket, a lovely bouquet of fresh flowers and a really nice travel bag. The gifts, along with all the good energy I received from everyone at Harpo, made me feel really welcomed and comfortable – as if I belonged.

It's Showtime

If you're young enough to believe those "Happily Ever After" fairy tales, the brutal truth in television is that it's often just an illusion, versus real life where it's practice that makes perfect. As is the case with TV wrestling, stunts also incorporate a bit of drama. For me, that meant infusing choreography into a short script.

I was told that Oprah will say, "Hi Angela." Then you'll say, "Hi Oprah" and wave to her. In the next segment you'll turn around, look into that camera and Oprah will say, "Angela, are you still there?" You'll say, "Yes I'm here." After that she'll say, "Come on down, I want to talk to you." You'll say, "Okay, Oprah. I'll be right there." Then you'll jump, explained one male producer.

Now on top of falling from the rooftop of a four-story building, landing precisely on the sweet spot of the air-bag below while taking into consideration all of the ever-changing last-minute instructions coming at me from left to right, I had lines to memorize. They were really determined to work "a sistah." And "a sistah" was equally as determined to be worked in exchange for a chance to sit with the Mighty O.

So, all through the practice jumps that took place minutes before the show I smiled and said to myself, "*I can do this.*"

But every now and then in television, Murphy's Law kicks in to create an embarrassing moment, as was the case during the half-time performance of Super Bowl XXXVIII, featuring the fabulous Janet Jackson. With the help of singer Justin Timberlake, one of "the girls" suddenly popped out the moment her performance ended. Millions around the world were watching. Some people thought little to nothing of it, while others were outraged – or at least they pretended to be.

I experienced a similar challenge, although not nearly as embarrassing as Jackson's. Still, it was a little too revealing for the producers, and me. Video shot during the practice jump revealed my long sleeve jersey blowing up and over my stomach. As a clever alternative, producers came up with a double-shirt design that would prevent anything from suddenly "popping out."

Next, the producers told me I hesitated before the practice jump. They explained how it happened: Right when Oprah was due to say, "Come on down" I was supposed to leap.

I knew exactly what they were referring to. Look before you leap was a totally natural reflex under such circumstances. And I can't really say that I was sorry. After all, it was my way of making sure that everyone – including me – had taken every precaution for my perfect landing.

The beauty of working with a qualified and competent team meant Rick placed an X on the exact spot of the rooftop ledge to note where I needed to stand to hit the sweet spot on the airbag below. Finally, all systems were finally ready and set to go.

In 3-2-1 ... GO!

"Places on the set," the director called.

The team and I hustled back onto the blustery rooftop so I could get into position to jump down and finally meet Oprah.

I must have lit up like a Christmas tree when I looked down and saw her looking up at me. This marked the first time I had seen her in person. Speaking of firsts, according to Oprah, this was the first time she had ever come outside the studio to open a live show at Harpo Studios. It was also the first time anyone had jumped off the roof of Harpo Studios as part of a segment of *"The Oprah Winfrey Show."* Still, to this day and likely for all of my life, I will always treasure the experience of appearing on the show as well as making history.

And there she was. ... Oprah Winfrey belted out, "We're live in Chicago, and I'm standing outside Harpo Studios. Way above me on our rooftop is Angela Meryl. Hi Angela," she said.

"Hi Oprah," I replied with a great big smile and a wave. Oprah continued. "She's about to do something that I must admit has me a little nervous. But she promises that this is just another day at the office for her. Why is there an ambulance standing by? Did I mention we're live in Chicago where today's show is all about dream jobs. And Angela says she loves every minute of her death-defying work."

That ended the first tease before my jump. From there I was escorted off the rooftop and taken downstairs to a beautiful lounge next to Oprah's office. Being there helped to keep me warm while watching other show guests talk about their dream jobs. Of particular recollection was a guest who was a cake maker and was moved to tears of joy by thoughts of his dad. It was at that point that I had to stop watching because I found myself becoming emotional with thoughts of my own dad, who I lost more than 15 years ago. Oh, how I only wish he could see me now.

I did my best to keep it together—emotionally speaking, quickly transitioning my thoughts to the sunset-colored walls. They were accented by some of the most beautiful African artwork I had ever seen.

"Oprah just redecorated this room," one of the producers said while noticing me staring in amazement. Before I could respond, I heard the words I had been waiting for: "Your segment is next, Angela."

In a flash, I was escorted back up to the ledge of the frigid rooftop, where I positioned myself on a spot marked with an X. Seconds later, I heard Oprah speaking to me from the warmth of her cozy studio as I stood there doing what little I could to keep warm and look fierce.

"Angela, are you still there?" she said."

"Yes, Oprah, I'm still here."

"Come on down. I want to talk to you."

"I'll be right there Oprah," I said.

In one fell swoop without any hesitation whatsoever, I turned, took one great big step away from the building and leaped off the roof.

For a split second, I found myself caught up in the enormously fluffy white clouds as if I was flying like a bird. As quickly as the thought entered my mind, Angela, the seasoned stuntwoman, knew to shift all attention to the tree staring straight ahead, knowing I was destined to land where and/or how my eyes were focused. At this point in my career there's no way I would ever want to be caught landing on my stomach from an awkward, self-imposed flip, all because I was focused elsewhere–especially, not on my big day with Oprah. No way!

I needed to fall on my back with knees slightly bent and chin tucked into my chest. That's the safest professional way for a stunt person to land without giving herself whiplash.

Especially for the viewers, I added more drama to the fall by kicking my legs and wildly flailing my arms to further excite the audience and leave them gasping for air, including my mom, who was sitting in the audience. She had no idea of the stunt I was to perform that day. Once she found out, I'm pretty sure she was the main one in the audience gasping for air. I could see her now, jumping to her feet and hollering at the top of her lungs, "My baby." But then too, I'd probably do the same if it was my child, while sensing the possibility of danger. With all of the those thoughts flashing through my mind at the speed of light, it took no more than a few blinks of an eye for me to land precisely on the X-spot of the airbag.

My first thought was "Ohmigod! I just jumped from Oprah's roof on live TV."

I popped up and said "Woohoo, I did it!"

That successful accomplishment left me feeling stronger and even more confident. The feeling in that moment reaffirmed what I already knew: Being a professional stuntwoman is my dream job!

Anyone other than a stunt person or daredevil at heart probably would never do what I do and would probably label me half crazy.

Rick and the ground crew were in place to ensure my safety during landing. Afterwards, I hugged and thanked them for helping to make the event yet another successful stunt in my career.

At a farther distance from me was the camera crew, whom I gave a big thumbs-up, thanking them for doing a great job and making it all look good.

Oprah and Angela

During the 90-second commercial break that began shortly after I rose from the fall, we trotted from the airbag to a holding area near the studio audience. A female sound technician placed one hand down my shirt to connect the microphone while hair and makeup crews worked quickly to make me presentable once again.

Through it all I tried calming myself for a chat with Oprah while moving at a super fast pace without a second to spare. Still, I noticed a piece of the microphone had snapped apart. Less than a second later, the sound technician scrambled to locate the missing part. Before I could take my next full breath she found it, snapped it back together and had me ready to go.

Next, we moved from the holding area to the stage while still out of focus from Oprah and the audience. Then Dean, Oprah's stage manager, positioned himself beside me. He prepared me to enter facing the audience. I peeped out at the audience, staring at all the faces captivated by the sound and thought of Oprah's introduction of the stunt-woman who had just jumped off the roof of the studio.

Hearing her refer to me as a "daredevil mom," and seeing the effect it had on the audience, was another surreal experience that brought a big ol' cheesy grin to my face.

While I was totally caught up in the moment, Dean suddenly leaned over and said, "Oprah wants you run out."

"OK," I said.

And no sooner than I answered, he tapped me and yelled, "Go, go, go!"

With a heart full of joy and a smile as bright as the sun I took off running onto the stage of "The Oprah Winfrey Show."

I was greeted with a standing ovation from hundreds of warm, smiling faces. Best of all, standing and smiling was the legendary Oprah Winfrey. It all sort of felt like being a little girl in a candy store, with permission from my mom to enjoy as much of the sugary treats as my stomach could stand.

Neither King Kong nor all the king's horses could have kept me from offering a great big hug to "her majesty" of daytime TV. And the billion-dollar lady reciprocated with a maternal embrace as if to say, "Well done Angela." That kind of support from such a remarkable and accomplished woman who is known for her undying efforts to inspire everyone to be their best is beyond explanation.

"Have a seat," she said.

Wasting no time at all, she went straight to the

A-list celebrities I've doubled: "Halle Berry, Beyoncé, Vivica

A. Fox," pausing in between each as if to allow me to confirm.

"Do you ever get scared," Oprah asked in a really girly kind of way.

"Yes. That was scary," I said. "But this is even scarier."

She laughed. I laughed. And the audience laughed, all of which really helped put me at ease during the dream interview.

Oprah's demeanor throughout the entire conversation was calm, cool and energetically friendly. She connected with me on a level that was pure and sincere. It felt as if she had known me forever. There is no wonder why so many people reveal their stories to her before any other media outlet. And to think that little ol' me, Angela Meryl from Willingboro, New Jersey, would be sitting on the same stage as the many other dignitaries, humanitarians and others who have made a difference in the lives of others. This was really mind-blowing.

In between the conversation, Oprah played an action packed clip from the compelling opening scene of "Kill Bill." In it, I delivered several power-packed blows to Uma Thurman before crashing through a glass table as the stunt double for Vivica A. Fox. This seemed to really impress Oprah and the audience.

We went on to talk about the experiences that inspired me to choose a career in stunts, as well as forewarnings from loved ones who would dare attempt a career such as mine. Of course I realized their fears are out of concern – with my best interests at heart. But for me, it's about following my heart, dreams and being passionate, rather than living vicariously through someone else's passion. Addressing Oprah and audience, I said, "As the expression goes: 'If you follow your passion, you'll never work a day in your life.' "

Oprah totally agreed.

The sit-down interview lasted about 10 minutes. When you add that to the show's opening and teasers between commercial breaks – when the cameras cut to me on the rooftop before Oprah finally called me to come down off the roof – my work seemed to dominate the episode even before I appeared onstage.

And to think all of this began during a year-end meeting with my publicist, who asked me to list my goals for the following year. One of my desires was to appear on *"The Oprah Winfrey Show."*

Mission accomplished.

I had the time of my life that day on "The Oprah Winfrey Show." My stunt took place during the eve of the finale season of the chart-topping daytime talk show in television history.

To this day, I still get full of excitement inside when I look at my picture with Oprah that sits on my desk. Often times when I examine the image, I am reminded of just how hungry, driven and focused I have always been on attaining success in the stunt business. Up until the time I appeared on "*Oprah*," rarely, if ever, did I pause to acknowledge the many accolades expressed by others over the years of my career. Instead, I focused my attention on doing the best job possible in hopes that the future would hold a place for me as a successful stuntwoman in Hollywood. Well, my dream came true. I paid for it with blood from time to time, a lot of sweat and a bucket full of tears over the years.

Feeling very validated, now is the time to answer the calls and questions when frequently approached by people who want to enter the business. About 99.9 percent of the time they have no clue how to break down the door of this tightly knit community.

Motivational speaker Greg Ketter once said, "When someone offers a suggestion or advice on how to do something, ask them; 1. Have you tried it. 2. Did it work for you." Now that I am in a position to answer yes to both questions, it's time to share the skills I've acquired with those standing on the outside of the door looking in.

Part One: My Beautiful Crash Landing

(Photo Credit: Shawn Barber)

CHAPTER 1

SETTING THE STAGE

(Photo Credit:
Shawn Barber)

~⊱⟨⟩⊰~

As a kid growing up in Willingboro, New Jersey, north of Philly, one calamity after another rocked my world. This proved to be perfect conditions for becoming a stunt performer. For example, I was sitting on the roof of my brother's friend's car when suddenly he slammed on the accelerator and I flew off the hood. Another time, I rode my bike downhill, made a sharp turn onto my street, and failed to notice a parked car. I rammed into it and flew over the hood for yet another crash landing.

Other snafus happened without me even leaving the ground, like when my older brother Craig and his friends would wrestle me into sweaty headlocks more times than I can count. As I squirmed to get free, our mother would scream, "Stop before someone gets hurt." This was warning that always seemed to come a little too late.

At Willingboro High School, which produced the legendary Olympian Carl Lewis, I not only ran track but endured a few tackles in what was supposed to be powder-puff football. But as graduation neared, I wanted to try activities where I did not end up with a mouthful of grass. In fact, I began to entertain the idea of a modeling or act-ing career. Being the think-it, do-it girl that I am, I began to get work in fashion shows and print ads. At one event, Philadelphia casting director Mike Lemon approached me and suggested that I take acting classes.

Mike's advice ignited a fire inside me, and I enrolled in a class that ultimately led me to audition for him and several other casting directors throughout the region. I began to book nonunion television commercials, which boosted my confidence and nudged me to take my act on the road to New York. There, I walked hour upon hour, dropping off headshots and résumés to every casting office that I could. Getting your foot in the door of many of these New York agencies was nearly impossible. They know that the multitudes flock to the city from near and far to try their luck on Broadway or in film, so some agents don't even bother to answer their doors.

But you can't keep a future stunt diva down. Here and there I began to receive calls for extra work on television shows and film productions. In fact, I found extra work to be a great way to learn the ropes, gain a better understand-ing of professional behavior on the set and pick up the lan-guage of the business.

To make ends meet financially, I worked as a model and/or make-up artist for a number of department stores. Sometimes, I was the annoying person at the counter trying to spray customers with perfume. I guess you could say that was the sweet smell of success.

CHAPTER 2

GETTING IN THE GAME

(Photo Credit:
Shawn Barber)

❦ ❭ ❦

L ate one night while working as an extra on the New York
set of 1995's "*Dead Presidents*," starring Larenz Tate, Keith
David and Chris Tucker, the production crew wanted to
push ahead and shoot the last few scenes necessary to stay
on track and on budget. But they had a problem: One of
the scenes required an experienced stunt driver, and they
didn't have one.

The assistant directors (AD) on the set were desperate.
They sent a production assistant (PA) to find someone with
a driver's license.

The production assistant entered the extras' holding area
and asked, "Does anyone have a valid driver's license?" I
raised my hand. (It would seem that there might be a lot of
people with a driver's license – but not so in New York City,
where people often rely on the subway to get around.)
Next, he asked, "Does anyone know how to drive in the
snow?"

As a Jersey girl who sledded through countless winters,
once ending up on someone's front lawn (Oops, never
told my mom that one – LOL). I raised my hand again. The

PA took me outside and verified my license was current. Afterward, he told the first assistant director (1st AD) that I was the one. The 1st AD's eyes widened.

"Come with me," he said, excitedly walking me toward a 1960s-style car. "Get in," he told me. Once I shut the door, he said, "OK, when you hear the word 'Action' I want you to drive down the street slowly, make a left turn and stop about 25 feet from the corner."

"Is that it?" I thought. And yes, it really was that simple. When the director called "Action," I drove down the street, made a left turn, and stopped 25 feet from the corner. For a split second as I sat in the car watching the other extras walk up and down the street behind Larenz, I wanted to be out there with them in hopes of getting more on-camera time. But when I thought about it again, I realized I was out of the frosty air, and the extras were trudging through bitter cold and snow. Meanwhile, I sat in a warm, cozy car. Stunt person or extra, I wondered to myself, "Hmmm." Afterward, the AD came over and said, "Nice job." I thanked him. Then it was back to "One" – the car's location at the top of the scene.

We did a few more takes before calling it a wrap. It was late and cold, and I was exhausted. So I hopped back on the bus to Jersey to rest for a few hours, only to rise again the next morning and head back to New York to beat the pavement in search of my next gig.

Fortunately all of my prospecting did not involve walking up and down the streets of Gotham. My friend Rusty McLendon used to stunt-double for actor-comedian Sinbad. He knew how much I wanted to become a member of the Screen Actors Guild (SAG) and asked if I would mind taking a fall on camera in a production where he was working. The job would qualify me for SAG membership, the coveted card every actor wants to score. The card means a higher pay rate, health insurance benefits and credit union membership. And that's just for starters. I thought, "All that for falling, when I'd fallen so many times as a kid, and got nothing *for my troubles but bloody knees.*" I then told Rusty, "No, I don't mind falling at all."

The moment I walked on set I felt the energy crackle. I'd stepped into the presence of many veteran stunt men and women. Even though they were very welcoming, I instantly felt intimidated.

Part of the job was simply to be a buffer: making sure the person who jumped from the "up" escalator and onto the "down" escalator didn't slip. The only problem was I wasn't on friendly terms with escalators. As a child, my shoelace got stuck in one, and the whole contraption had to be turned off to free me. I have approached them with trepidation ever since and still do to this day.

For this stunt, once the director called "Action" I had to jump from where I was positioned on a ledge in order to buffer a 200-pound man attempting to jump off one escalator and onto another. It was daunting to be responsible for somebody else's safety. But I went to my old standbys: focus and prayer. I also visualized a successful outcome and repeatedly told myself, "*I can do this. I can do this. I can do this.*" And sure enough, I did it.

By the end of the job, I was eligible to join SAG through a process known as Taft-Hartley. The term has a special meaning to film and television actors who are not in the union. Those who become a "principal performer," by saying a line or performing a stunt in a SAG production are immediately eligible to join the union and covered under the SAG contract with the production company for 30 days – at which point the person must either join SAG or cease working on union productions. Once a person joins the union, he or she is not supposed to work on any non-union productions, per the terms of the by-laws. For more information, go to www. sag.org.

Though I was now eligible, I didn't join within those first 30 days because I was still scraping by, working at department stores and performing as an extra. On top of that, I wasn't sure I was ready.

Working on "*New York Undercover*," a prime-time television series that aired in the '90s, helped build my confidence. It all started with a phone call out of the blue from the show's stunt coordinator Pete Bucossi. He said he'd heard I was a pretty good driver from the first assistant director on "*Dead Presidents*."

Pete said, "I need a female driver to double for Lauren Velez as she pulls away from a curb." Velez played Nina Moreno, a fellow detective and love interest to Detective Eddie Torres (Michael DeLorenzo), who was the partner of Detective J.C. Williams (Malik Yoba).

"I can do it," I said. I was certain that it would be no problem – until he asked if I was SAG. "No," I told him. He seemed a little disappointed at first. But then I told him I was SAG eligible. So he asked once more if I were interested. At the time, I told him the truth: "Not really."

Now he was doubly disappointed because he had an African-American woman who could perform stunts and was SAG eligible. That wasn't so easy to find back then. We ended the call with him suggesting that I think about it some more.

Looking back, I've come to realize that the fear of the unknown was holding me hostage. In other words, the thing standing between me and my plum job was not the $1,180 annual SAG membership fee. Instead, it was me. A few weeks later, Pete called again and asked if I were interested in doing stunts for "*New York Undercover*." Again I said "no." But I had to admit that I certainly had the background for it, having grown up as a tomboy and later acquiring martial arts skills that included Tang Soo Do, Goju and Taekwondo. Master Andrew Walker, my Taekwondo and Shotokan instructor in Philadelphia, always believed that a woman should be able to protect herself at all times. I trained under his instruction about four times a week. Classes would sometimes last three hours at a time, especially during the summer when many of the younger students were out of school.

There, in the basement of Kingsessing Recreational Center, Master Walker taught us various Taekwondo forms, or imaginary choreographed fights against multiple people. We learned self-defense techniques that included disarming a person with a knife or a gun, grappling and more. Soon after I got a third call from the "New York Undercover" stunt coordinator. By this time, I felt maybe there was a reason he kept calling.

Was this God telling me what to do? Pete's calls were offering work – a job. On top of that, over and over, he kept telling me that (at the time) there were no other black stunt women actively involved in the stunt business. Sure, there was Kym Washington. But she was always gone, doubling for Whoopi Goldberg. So in that moment, I guess he just caught me on the right day, at the right time and I accepted his offer with a very gracious yes. I had no idea for sure where it would take me. I didn't even know how much work I was going to get out of New York Undercover – if any besides that one job. But right then I began to think that maybe this could be my new career. It sure paid more than extra work and was a lot more fun and exciting.

Days afterward I was on set doing my first stunt: doubling a 60-year-old woman who gets shot accidentally. To have a sense of how she would fall, I watched her the entire morning: how she held her hands, her head, the way she walked. I thought of my grandparents – how they walk and the way they take their time getting from place to place. Younger people might be able to catch themselves before they fall, but older people are going down. I wanted to capture the woman's physicality as I doubled for her at the moment the bullet supposedly struck and crumpled her body. After working on a few episodes of "New York Undercover," I discovered that my SAG membership made it possible for me to visit the SAG office for a monthly production report. The report names the film and TV projects being shot around town and the production office addresses – along with the names of the stunt coordinators.

Every day, I reviewed the lists of shoots and then went to the production office to drop off headshots and résumés. For every job I got, I sent a postcard with my latest gig on it, announcing to stunt coordinators, *"Hey, I'm working,"* in hopes of positioning myself for the next gig.

Though I tried to resist it, it seemed that my destiny would involve all the bumps and bruises of my youth: riding bikes, getting put in choke holds, crash landings and more. At least at this stage of the game I would be well-compensated for it. That's it. I am a stuntwoman.

After the first few years, I realized that I had to retire as an extra to be taken seriously as a stuntwoman. There were just so many hours in the day, so I put time and effort into advancing my stunt career: calling stunt coordinators, mailing or dropping off headshots and résumés. I figured the universe doesn't know what to give you if you have your hand in too many pots.

Still I continued to accept work as an extra on television commercial gigs because they pay well. As a union background worker, you earned $200 or above for eight hours, and then if you worked longer you got overtime. Bring your clothes? If you did, that was an extra $17 a day for maintenance. Work in the rain or walk through smoke? That was another $17 each. For a 12-hour day, you could easily make $500. If you got upgraded to principal, that was an even better pay scale. Then there were the residuals from commercials, which meant more money every time it aired on television. Many people live on residuals. For the rest of us, it's money that keeps us afloat between jobs. I worked as an extra on many commercials but tried to avoid the ones with stunts because I didn't want stunt coordinators to see me as an extra and not give me higher paid stunt work. By my fourth year in the game, I was a regular on the New York film scene. But I wondered if I could make it in Los Angeles – thousands of miles from family, home, friends and the condo I'd just purchased. With two stunt friends in Los Angeles and another buddy who agreed to let me sleep on his sofa, I was eager to discover everything I could about doing stunts the Hollywood way.

My friend Brennan Dyson, who doubles LL Cool J on the CBS hit series *"NCIS Los Angeles,"* took me around to a few sets and introduced me to the art of hustling. At Hjelte Sports Center in Encino – an affluent suburb northwest of Los Angeles, I met people who played in a Saturday base-ball league. It was a great place to develop relationships because everyone was there to have a good time, but they were also stunt people. There, you could meet them and get your hustle on, and no one felt pressured. After two months in Los Angeles, I decided I wasn't ready for such a drastic change and returned home for two years, continuing to work as a stunt woman and make-up artist in department stores. But I kept up my hustle. Whenever a Los Angeles-based stunt coordinator came through town, I made it a point to get on set and get hired so that I could add his or her name to my résumé. I figured that when I ulti-mately returned to L.A., it would give me more creditability.

CHAPTER 3

TO THE NEXT LEVEL

(Photo Credit:
Shawn Barber)

❧ ❭ ❧

One Sunday morning in September 2000, I woke up feeling it was time to go to Los Angeles for good. I rented a room instead of an apartment, found a kennel for my dog, Diva (a black chow) – that was way too big to impose on friends – and had someone house-sit my condo in case things didn't pan out.

Two weeks later, I was in Los Angeles. The initial months were tough. I was scared, homesick, getting lost on the freeways and racking up a ton of parking tickets. But I stuck it out, trusting the tide would turn if I continued to hustle by contacting every stunt coordinator in town. That's when the business of hustling took over my life. For me, it was the combination of training, marketing and promoting myself while diligently studying acting for eight straight months. Then finally, I got my first job in L.A. On the hit TV series, "*VIP*," starring Pamela Anderson, I doubled an actress in a real girlie kind of fight. Based on my résumé alone, stunt coordinator Jeff Cadiente really took a chance on the new girl in town, which is how I got the job. That's when I really committed to the city and signed a lease on an apartment. It wasn't the nicest part of town, but it was a roof over my head and a place all my own where I could bring my dog. A couple of months down the road, I got a call from Bill, of Bill's Stunts. The call came in the middle of an acting class, but fortunately we were on break. "Hey kiddo," he said, "Jeff Imada is looking for you. He said for you to go to the set of 'The Time Machine' now! They're looking for a girl to double the lead actress, Samantha Mumba."

I had no idea who Samantha Mumba was. But the fact that this was a chance to double a lead actress was a big deal for me. So, I left class right away and drove straight to the set.

When I got there, a production assistant took me to Jeff, a Los Angeles-based stunt coordinator who I had once met in New York. He gave me the once-over then asked if I knew martial arts. No sooner than I said yes, he had four stuntmen attack me just to see how well I could defend myself. One by one they approached me. My job was to disarm them, whether that meant a fake kick in the stomach, a blow to a thigh or a punch toward the face. I made it look so believable that all Jeff could say was, "OK, go see Hair, Makeup and Wardrobe. If they approve, the job is yours."

So off I went to Hair and Makeup. With a wig, they said, I would be good to go. The clothes for the part were baggy, so being an exact body double for the lead actress wasn't crucial.

During the shoot, which lasted about two months in the dry, brittle desert, I had to run all day with the sun beaming down on me in temperatures above 90-degrees Fahrenheit. Take after take, I had to jump into a monster's arms – a costume worn by a stuntman – and then the two of us got sucked into a big hole, with a truckload of sand rushing in after us. We had to keep our eyes and mouths closed. After each take, they whisked off sand from us with an air canister. We were to blow our noses, drink water and spit the excess sand out. It was like being buried alive – only standing up.

I went from surviving suffocation to crashing through glass when I doubled for Vivica A. Fox in *"Kill Bill."*

Director Quentin Tarantino had been casting *"Kill Bill"* for three weeks before I even heard the job existed. And at the time I was just coming off of hernia surgery. A hernia is an opening or weakness in the muscular structure of the wall of the abdomen. This defect causes a bulging of the abdominal wall. Imagine a barrel with a hole in its side and a balloon that is blown up inside the barrel. Part of the inflated balloon would bulge out through the hole. The balloon going through the hole is like the tissues of the abdomen bulging through a hernia.

My type of hernia was called inguinal. It had no direct relation to any particular stunt I had performed. Instead, the list of possibilities included predisposed tissue and was most likely worsened by heavy lifting, vigorous exercise, straining and more.

The day I got home from the hospital, I got a call from the assistant stunt coordinator – Kenny Lesco, who had been desperately trying to find my contact information so that I could come in for an audition. I didn't know much about the project, but was told that it involved fighting. That made me think to bring my karate teacher, Marcus.

Marcus Salgado is known for having trained Wesley Snipes for many years. As you may know, Snipes started out as a kid and went on to earn a 5th Dan Black Belt in Shotokan Karate. His skills as a badass are showcased in such action-adventure films as the *"Blade"* trilogy, *"Passenger 57"* and *"Demolition Man"* with Sylvester Stallone. Since I couldn't drive due to multiple incisions, Marcus was the perfect one to go with me. After we arrived, Kenny introduced us to Quentin Tarantino, who looked at me as if he were sizing me up to see if I could handle the demands of the role he'd created. He said the fight scenes would be lowdown and dirty, not lightweight and girly.

I had to be honest with Quentin and tell him I had hernia surgery the day before. I went as far as showing him my gauze bandages. He could see that I was in no condition to work right then. Because I knew I could quickly regain my strength, I pleaded with him to give me a week to heal. I promised that I would come back and show him what I could do. In reality, I knew that it would take weeks, possibly even months, to heal. But I really wanted that job! Quentin said he'd give me a week to heal and return to audition. I was totally ecstatic when he said that. It meant the chance to work with him in a lowdown dirty fight on film. On top of that, if I got the job, I'd be doubling Vivica A. Fox. That would have been a first for me.

Marcus and I left immediately so I could go home to rest. When I got there I basically collapsed. As exhausted as I was, a countless number of karate moves began scrolling through my head at the speed of a million miles per minute. While basically confined to the bed that week, all I could do was think and talk on the phone. So, my karate instructor and I talked through the different combinations of jabs, punches and uppercuts that we would do on the day of the audition.

Against doctor's orders, I went in to see Quentin the following week with a sore and stapled stomach. I had to show him and his crew that I could hit back with fierce intensity, strength and control. I followed Marcus's directions as he called out combinations for me to execute. Then I did a small fight sequence against three team members of Master Yuen Woo-Ping's Beijing fight team. The guys threw a couple of punches, one of which appeared to knock me out. As sore and stitched up as I was, I stayed on top of my game and fell dramatically to the floor in true show-biz style. Yeah, I was determined to get that job.

Master Yuen is one of the most coveted fight-scene choreographers in the industry. His film credits include *"The Matrix"* and *"Crouching Tiger, Hidden Dragon."* Some say Master Yuen's work on *"The Matrix"* set a whole new standard for cinematic fight scenes. With all that said, I was really eager to work with the two film icons – Master Yuen and Quentin. After the fight, I walked off the mat and over to Marcus. His first words were "nice job." Then he told me that Vivica and Master Yuen had both been watching. He said Vivica clapped, while Master Yuen walked around the mat, nodding his head as if he were pleased. As I was about to leave, the second assistant director came over and told me, "You got the job."

"Ohmigod!" I almost screamed aloud when he said that. I mean this was the most challenging preparation of my career at that time – mentally speaking. On top of that, my body was physically less than its best while trying to recover from the recent surgery. Despite all that, he still said, "You got the job." Seriously, I'm not sure I could ever put into words what I felt at that moment. What I can say is that once the shock wore off I knew this job would be a game changer for my career.

After that, I could not wait to thank Quentin. He told me he could see the determination in my face. But what impressed him the most was that I brought my karate instructor along.

Most of the production team was now ready to leave for a two-month stay in Beijing. Thank God that none of what they were planning to shoot in China involved Vivica's character in any fights. That meant I didn't have to go. By the time they returned, it was on and popping. We began training for three straight weeks with the Beijing fight team in preparation of the opening scene. I did 10 sets of 10 jumps daily, leaping into the air while bringing my knees up to my chest as high as I could. I did this so that when we shot the scene, I'd be able to jump backward, clear a couch, then come crashing through a glass table. Of course that meant crashing through at least *two* glass tables, since directors rarely settle for one take.

All of this was extremely grueling on a girl. In fact, one day I went home crying because I was in so much pain. When I returned the next day I asked the assistant stunt coordinator why they picked me. He said "because Master Yuen thought that you could be trained." When I heard that the tears went away and the real martial artist in me came out in full force. I jumped, stretched, fought – and I quit bitching so that I could focus on learning what Master Yuen had to teach me.

The scene that made it into the movie opens with Uma's character punching Vivica's character in the face. Vivica quickly recovers and throws Uma Thurman into the wall. Uma comes back at her again. As Vivica's double, I did all the dangerous stuff, including an ax kick to Uma's face. Uma then grabbed my foot and shoved it up and away. That sent me flying backward over the couch, landing on the glass table and crashing through it.

Take One didn't go as planned. Something went wrong with the glass. So for take two, I'm secretly thinking, "Man, I *really don't want to do this again. I could break my neck if I don't land right*". But I kept my fears to myself and got back into position at the top of the scene. With Take Two, I heard

"Action," leaped over the couch onto the table and landed on the glass, which shattered as I hit the floor. Unbeknownst to me, when the scene was done, I was bleeding badly. Before I realized it, medic Tony Evans had rushed in. He ushered me over to the kitchen sink on the set. The pointer finger on my right hand was gushing blood. Like any seasoned stunt person, I knew in the back of my mind that there was a good chance of getting cut in this scene. Once I stopped to think to think about, it all became clear to me. The table I went through was made out of tempered glass, which breaks into big chunks, unlike candy glass, which breaks into smaller, finer pieces. That explained it. Tony said, "If I can't stop the bleeding, we're going to have to take you to the hospital."

"But, but, but ... I gotta walk my dog, I told him, and what about my car? Who's going to drive it home? He said, "No buts. We're going to the hospital." So we got into a van and went to the hospital, where I got three stitches. Later that night, Keith Adams, the coordinator, called to see if I could return to work the next day. I quickly said, "Hell yeah." As hard as I had worked to get that job, I wasn't about to give it up because of a few stitches.

At work the next day, my finger continued to bleed. Between you, me and the pages of this book, I believe it was because the other actor involved in the scene was more focused on her work than on my finger, which I completely understood. So I sucked it up and kept going. If I could soldier through hernia surgery, what were a few stitches in my finger, right? You've got to be like an NFL player in this business – perform even when you're hurt at times, while keeping your eyes on the goal.

After we wrapped my scenes, everybody clapped for me. That's when Quentin came over and gave me the biggest hug. He kissed me on the lips, which I thought was hilarious. Then the 1st AD chased me around the set trying to squirt me with his water bottle.

The icing on the cake came at the 2004 World Taurus Stunt Awards.

There, Quentin publicly thanked me for making the first 10 minutes of his movie come alive. Zoe Bell, who doubled for Uma, and I got nominated for "Best Fight" scene. I was also nominated for "Best Overall Stunt By a Woman." Although neither of us won, being nominated in a fight category dominated by men was a huge honor.

In 2009, I was recognized once again. This time I was the recipient of a Diamond in the Raw Award, during a ceremony that celebrates "The Achievements of Hollywood's Most Precious Gem: The Stuntwoman."

In May 2010, I got even more love when Heather Vandrell and I were awarded The World Taurus Stunt Award for "Best Overall Stunt By A Woman" for our work in "Obsessed," where I doubled for Beyoncé Knowles.

Though much of the work I do is intended to hide me, being nominated for and receiving awards were proof that others were watching and had some sense of appreciation for the expertise I brought to the game.

Part Two: Making it Happen For You

(Photo Credit: Russell Baer)

CHAPTER 4

THE BEAUTY OF A MENTOR

(Photo Credit:
Shawn Barber)

❦ ⟩ ❦

" **A**lways remember your mentor and who brought you up into this business. They are the ones who got you where you are today. You find out real fast who your true friends are when BAD things happen. Those are the ones you want to surround yourself with. It's a tough business, and you should take it seriously, explained fellow stuntman Hiro Koda, in an article appearing at iStunt. com. Koda's credits as a stunt coordinator include his work on the set of Nickelodeon's "Supah Ninjas!" and as a fight consultant for "Sherlock Holmes: A Game of Shadows." It is really to your advantage to have a mentor in this business – someone with more experience in the game than you.

With nearly two decades in the business, I thought it best to write a book that would help guide you based on my success. Wherever you are in the world, try your best to use the suggestions throughout this book and locate other stunt people in your area for hands-on guidance.

I am fortunate to have several mentors, including Jalil Jay Lynch, who has been here to guide me from the very start of my career. As one of the most sought-after drivers in the stunt business, his career began as the double for Chris Rock, in the movie *"New Jack City"* (1991). Jay's driving and riding skills are constantly showcased in action-packed movies such as *"Torque"* (2004), in which he valiantly rode a motorcycle for a spectacular jump from a freestyle moto-cross ramp onto the top of a moving train, then riding off the locomotive as it barreled down the tracks behind him as he sped off in a fury – doubling actor Ice Cube. I could easily go on and on telling you about some of the breath-taking stunts of this legendary performer.

After uprooting from New York to Los Angeles, there were times when the never-ending grind became frustrating. The biggest frustration of all was in not knowing when my next job was coming. I had money coming in from residuals and unemployment during the weeks when I had no other income sources or work. Getting the next job so I could continue to prove myself was very important to me, as was balancing my budget and spending.

Jay advised me to stay on a budget on limiting my social activities: forgoing movies, dinner and even that new pair of jeans – so that I wouldn't have to be saddled with a 9-to-5. Sure it would have been much easier to have a steady job and no stress, but that wasn't my vision.

He'd say, "This biz is not for everyone!" By that he meant that I needed to have the passion for the craft, versus a passion for money. He'd tell me, "Hustle, hustle, hustle, then go to the beach and regroup for a few days. After that, it's back to the hustle." And that's exactly what I did. Jay had a unique way of dealing with his troubles and offered a special kind of therapy to all of his close friends. "If you get stressed," he'd say, "take out The Z." The Z was his 1987 Chevy Camaro Z-28, with a 350 horsepower tuned port-fuel injected engine, oversized tires and chrome rims. That car was hot and could really haul ass.

At times when I'd bitch and complain about my issues in the business, Jay would say, "Angela, get in The Z!" Seconds later, we'd be drifting (meaning traveling sideways) down the middle of a two-way street burning rubber in a full-on power slide that would send us 250 feet down the block before drifting into three to four doughnuts or 360-degree spins. We would exit the spin with the same power, head sideways down the block all over again, perform a 180-degree turn and land in the same parking spot where we started. This kind of crazy, warp-speed driving – which back then we'd do in desolate areas far outside of city – would always take my mind off everything, including my problems. Nowadays, you'll get arrested for doing dough-nuts in a parking lot. So, by all means, please don't try it.

Having such a great mentor also has made me a more marketable driver. For example, on rainy days, my mentor would sometimes take me out to some desolate areas and teach me how to power slide around corners and do 90- and 180-degree turns, along with reverse 180s. He would demonstrate them first, then switch seats to coach me through it. His theory was that if I could drive really well in "The Z" then I could drive really well in anything. Can you see how beneficial it is to your career to have a genuine and true friend as a mentor?

Before we go into the next section, I'd like to stress again that you do not try what I did back then to release frustra-tions. Things are far different now, as opposed to when I got started in the business. If driving at warp speed is a skill you wish to perfect or a means of easing your mind, take my advice and visit one of the many great stunt-driving schools. There, under the direction of an expert you can perfect your skills. If you don't know of any, don't worry. I've made some available to you in the resource guide at the back of the book.

CHAPTER 5

SETTING YOURSELF APART

(Photo Credit:
Shawn Barber)

⚬⟨⟩⚬

They say hindsight is 20/20. So if I had to do it all over again, I would definitely start out by training in gymnastics to gain a competitive edge. Gymnastics will give you a better awareness of your body, which will be quite helpful when the job calls for low falls, high falls, ratchets, air rams, street fights and martial arts. Gymnastics looks great on a resume too!

I created a niche for myself as a stunt driver and a precision driver. To be the best at it can assure me of work well into retirement if I choose, which is not too common for the average stunt person who takes the bumps, bruises and falls the job requires.

If you have a broad knowledge of cars, quick reflexes and good driving skills, you could become a stunt driver, which is one of my areas of specialty. Stunt driving is the more dramatic style of driving that makes television and film appear far more spectacular.

For you to deliver a spectacular performance every time, there is no way around the ongoing process of stunt-driving courses. Start early in your career because perfection requires many years of behind the wheel experience. You'll also need to learn precision-driving. Precision-driving is used most often in television commercials where you'll need to hit the mark every time in order to keep working and be in demand.

Stunt driving programs include sessions in the classroom and behind the wheel. They'll teach you how to slide, hit a mark, and perform 90-, 180- and 360-degree turns. Years ago it was as simple as rigging the parking brake or taking out a fuse to get the car to do what was necessary to accomplish the stunt. But with today's technology, even the most basic stunts may require a lot more consideration of the big picture.

There are some really great instructors in the business to demonstrate what it takes to get a car to obey your command. Rick Seaman's and Bobby Ore's driving schools are among my favorites on the west coast. On the east coast, Roy Farfel owns another amazing driving school. Roy and I worked together on one of my first car commercials in New York, where I mostly sat back, listened and learned. Although I was the right body type for the job and could do all of the driving, no one on the set seemed to have confidence in my ability or skills.

Sometimes you will work with a production company that knows exactly what it wants but lacks the time or inclination to communicate it to you. That was exactly the case with one commercial, in particular. Whenever "Action" was called, I would do as told. Unfortunately, the director never seemed to feel it was "hot" enough. Hot is code for fast, which meant they wanted me to speed up. However, they did let me drive through a dark, smoky passage on the sidewalk beneath New York's South Street Seaport. That suggested they had a good degree of confidence in me. Through it all, I seized the opportunity to further perfect my driving skills. I also realized that it's not good to complain. Thank God I got paid for the day's work and earned residual income each time the commercial aired.

Gotta love that. If you want to achieve success driving in television commercials, you need to be able to establish a steady speed and hit a mark, because the director often wants to capture the same shot from a series of angles. For that, you've got to hold it steady anywhere from 5 miles per hour to 65 miles per hour – moment after moment as the camera truck (also known as the "Russian arm" or "process truck") drives in front, alongside and behind you. Maintaining a steady speed seems easy enough, but few of us do it when we're in our own cars. Believe me, it's an acquired skill.

Once I did a commercial that was a real nail-biter. It was on a two-lane mountain road with plenty of curves, in Truckee, California. The location was gorgeous but with little room for error. One wrong move and either I was going over the cliff or running over the crew.

First I had to drive through a rain machine to give the impression that the action was happening at night during a downpour. Then as the scene began I was instructed to come in "hot," hit the guardrail with the right front quarter panel of the car and continue to slide along the rail for a few feet before finally pulling away. After that, I had to slow to a stop so as not to slide over the cliff where there was no guardrail.

When director Simon West called "Action" I started off about 40 miles per hour on the first take. Afterward, stunt coordinator Brent Fletcher came up to me and asked if I could go any faster, as apparently 40 miles per hour was too slow for the director. From that point forward I came in at a roaring 60 miles per hour instead. There were many other factors that went into making that commercial – way too many to list – and I had to do them all much faster on every take.

Developing one or more areas of expertise is likely to contribute greatly to your success in the stunt business. Here is a list of many of the most popular areas to establish and develop your skills…

- Gymnastics
- Motorcycles – on and off road
- Car work
- Wire work
- Scuba diving, surfing, swimming
- Firearms
- Squibs, or packs of fake blood that attach to your body to detonate at an appointed time
- Horseback riding
- Rappelling down mountains, the side of buildings, or out of airborne helicopters
- Ratchet: a harness rigged to a wire that yanks a stunt person through the air similar to being thrown from an explosion
- High falls (above 30 feet/3 stories) and low falls (under 30 feet)
- Mini trampolines
- Fire burns (full and partial body)
- Martial Arts
- Hand-to-hand combat, fist fighting
- Parkour and free-running – running from structure to structure with flips and acrobatics along the way
- Air rams – a pneumatic device that catapults a stunt person through the air

The areas where you are most passionate will probably become your areas of expertise. I've practiced a lot of driving stunts over the years, which makes me good with cars. I also love martial arts, so I'm a natural when it comes to fight scenes. That's why I got excited when I saw the stunt breakdown for 2009's "*Obsessed,* "a film starring Beyoncé and Idris Elba. It basically said: "Housewife kicks girlfriend's ass."

Although I knew little else about the job, I knew to show up for the audition in high heels, low-rise jeans and a cute T-shirt that showed cleavage – something you might see Beyoncé wear. I also fixed my hair and makeup similar to how she would look. I needed them to envision me as her double.

I figured my chances of getting the gig were strong. I had already doubled for Beyoncé in "*Austin Powers in Goldmember* "and a couple of commercials, including one for Pepsi, in which my task was to drive an Aston Martin a few feet alongside a gas pump and stop. Why couldn't Beyoncé have done that herself? Because it takes a precision driver to stop on the same mark, take after take.

On the set of "*Obsessed,*" I met up with stunt coordinator Lance Gilbert, who took me to talk to the director. That was unusual. Things don't usually happen in that order. Instead, more often you are taken to hair and make-up to determine if your complexion and bone structure are a workable match. Then it's off to wardrobe, where it's best to be smaller than the actress, because when you put on butt, hip and thigh pads, you will appear to be the same size. Chances are, if all goes well the job is yours. Lance and I sat down with the director and showed him my résumé, along with some photos I had previously taken with Beyoncé. Using his phone, Lance then forwarded a link to my Web site to the director and also one of the producers so they could actually see some of my work, particularly the fight scene from "*Kill Bill.*" Shortly thereafter, I got word that the job was mine.

Together with Lance and stuntwoman Heather Vandrell (who doubled for co-star Ali Larder), we choreographed the big knockdown, drag-out fight scene in various segments. We started off in the bedroom, where the three of us created scenarios to suggest what would happen between two women going at it in the bedroom. The director and executive producer watched and weighed in.

"We like this, but change that."

Afterward, Beyoncé and Ali came in and rehearsed what we had choreographed. They were to fight from the bedroom to the bathroom, back to the bedroom, through the hallway, down the stairs and up to the attic. It was a multi-room beat down.

When it was time to shoot the actual scenes things were still changing and being locked into place. The floor was padded for Beyoncé and Ali to run through their dialogue and fall, after which the director would call "Cut!" The padding was then removed for Heather and me to step in for the actual fight. The two of us went at it for eight to 10 hours a day for three weeks straight and both dropped a ton of weight.

One day between shots in the bathroom scene, Beyoncé stood at the door as I was seated on the floor near the tub. "May I tell you something," I asked her.

"Sure," she said.

"I'm so proud of you," I told her. "I've watched you grow from singing in Destiny's Child to acting in "Austin Powers," where I was also your stunt double.

"Ohmigod!" she said. "That's right. It was you. I forgot you'd done 'Austin Powers.'"

"And the Pepsi commercial," I said.

"Thank you, thank you so much," Beyoncé said. Then the first AD called the set to order, and it was time to get back to kicking ass.

Ever consider working at an amusement park or circus? Their live shows are an excellent way to strengthen and perfect your stunts skills while earning income at the same time. Of course, you'll need to walk in the door with some type of talent, whether it's fighting, gymnastics, motorcycles, high falls, etc. If you land the job, consider it a great place to practice, especially if you're not very seasoned in front of the camera or a live audience. There, you can also build on your technique, group interaction and safety skills, all of which are crucial to a Hollywood stunt performer. Your performance could vary from day to day which would be like performing in a television or film production, where things tend to change. Something as simple as your cue coming a split second early or late could cause injury either to you or someone on the set. Learning to adapt to the potential changes will help further develop your skills as a seasoned stunt professional.

The work might even be seasonal in some locations, such as the summer carnivals in the U.S. There's also the opportunity for domestic or foreign travel to exotic destinations such as Japan, Italy and Paris. It's a good way to get footage for your reel so you can present yourself to stunt coordinators. Perform an online search of amusement parks and circuses. Check their Web sites to learn the schedule for auditions, which are also listed on what is called the Stunt Contact. I'll tell you more about that in an upcoming chapter.

CHAPTER 6

PLAY SAFE AND GO HOME

(Photo Credit:
Shawn Barber)

⟶❧ ⟩ ❧⟵

C ircumstances leading to the possibility of injury are inevitable in the business of stunts. I can recall several instances where I came so close to injury, including on the set of *"Pirates of the Caribbean: At World's End."* Standing 40 feet above ground along the very edge of a platform, our stunt crew waited to be secured into harnesses so we could be hung from the side of the ship. Suddenly, two of the wheels under the platform collapsed. Everyone on the platform either fell to their knees or on their butts before scrambling to safety. Luckily, no one was hurt and no one took the plunge to the concrete four stories below.

Between you and me, though, while that was a great job, it wasn't always a comfortable. The costume I had to wear each day included a very snug and fitted corset. On top of that, I wore a harness for security during some of the stunts. I was breast feeding at the time, which meant that I needed to either feed my child or pump the milk every couple of hours. Not pumping would lead to swelling as the breast became engorged with milk. Therefore, the swelling would cause the alreadysnug costume and harness to become downright tight. At times, that led to a cross between discomfort and extreme pain. So, in reality, we all didn't escape agony. Then there was the time I flipped an ambulance on the set of "Grey's Anatomy."

For that particular episode, I was asked to T-bone an ambulance. That meant to brutally crash one ambulance into the side of another. For budgetary reasons, this is a one-shot take. The lead-up to the crash was taped on the studio lot where the series is shot.

With tires screeching, I drove around the corner about 45 miles per hour, which does not sound that fast until you've taken into consideration the force of the ambulance created by the weight and other factors. On top of that, I had to drive sandwiched between two buildings with little to no wiggle room, and appear to recklessly approach the crowd of lead actors before crashing into another ambulance. That was some serious precision driving.

While putting on my hard-shell rollerblading knee-pads in preparation for the second part of the stunt, I was approached by the stunt coordinator's assistant. "Here, use my hockey knee pads," he said. "You're going to need something a whole lot bigger and stronger since there is a great chance that the motor could get shoved into your knees."

"WHAT!" I thought.

He also wore Nomex fire safety gear. Now mind you, he wasn't driving in the scene like me. He was in charge of fire safety. That meant being prepared for the worst possibility, including a real rescue.

A voice within then spoke to me. "Hmmm, should I have mine on???" But then I remembered being told I didn't need fire-safety gear because either the fuel had been removed from the ambulance I was to collide into or it had a fuel-cell installed in the rear with a limited amount of gas in the tank.

More and more I got excited as stunt coordinator Kerry Rosall explained exactly where he wanted the ambulances to collide. He then waited until I had my helmet on before issuing one last reminder: "Be sure to hit the door of the ambulance. Otherwise, if you miss and hit the cable, it could snap off, whip around, come straight at you through the front windshield and decapitate you."

The cable he was referring to was attached to the ambulance on one end and a crane on the other end to help the ambulance flip over on impact.

"Once you pass the green screen I want you to floor it," Kerry instructed.

The green screen was there to simulate a hospital setting, creating the illusion that the entire scene was taking place in the parking lot of a medical facility. To the average person, all of this might sound a little scary. But the stuntwoman in me thought *"Wow, I get to wreck two trucks and not get a ticket or increased insurance rates. Woohoo!"*

I floored it when the director yelled "Action," charging right into the side of the ambulance. But, for some reason, the vehicle did not flip over.

I sat in the driver's seat looking at the other ambulance and wondering what happened? *"Did I do something wrong?"* I wondered. Nope. As instructed, the stunt was executed perfectly on my end. The problem was that the cable snapped. I just thank God it didn't whip around and come through the windshield. That, my friends, is a perfect example of the importance of doing everything you are supposed to do – exactly the way you are told to do it. From time to time in this business, someone *does* get hurt. Once, I got kicked in the face by an actress on a set. In the scene, she was supposed to lie face down on a flight of stairs, then turn and *appear* to kick me in the face. Though I had asked her to make eye contact first, she forgot and kicked me squarely in the nose. That sent me flying to the bottom of the stairs. Fortunately, it didn't break my nose or give me a black eye. For that, I considered myself lucky enough to return to work the next day. Remember, there is *always* someone on the sidelines or a phone call away that's ready to take your place and get cozy with the actor you're doubling.

Now, I'd like to share some tried-and-proven techniques of my own and a few others from several highly acclaimed stunt colleagues and friends in the business. Listed, as follows, they should prove very useful to you.

Safety Tips for Successful Fighting

Fighting is like a dance. There's a beat to every movement. Find your groove in it, and stay on it. Keep your eyes open at all times, and always be sure to make eye contact before taking action. Distance is another important factor as well. Fight scenes are dangerous and look fake if not properly executed. If you deliver a believable kick/punch and the other person's reaction is too fast or too slow, it looks staged. It's absolutely critical that you demonstrate the body's precise reaction when on the receiving end of a kick or punch. You can even exaggerate a bit for the camera to help capture a really dramatic impact.

In a real-life street fight the intent is for someone to get hurt. But when a stunt person fights on camera, the clear objective is to walk away without a scratch. For this to work, you've got to keep a safe distance from other actors in the scene. Most stunt people know this. Unfortunately, newcomers tend to get a bit overzealous from time to time. A wrong move can cost you a paycheck, your health and, perhaps, your life.

The person appearing to be punched or slapped must react at the *precise* time a hand crosses the bridge of the nose. For "street cred" (credibility), your head must also snap back to reflect the impact of the slap or punch. This is particularly effective for people with long, full hair. The hair greatly enhances the visual effect. Similarly, a real kick in the stomach would make the average person double over in pain. As the stunt person, you have to mimic that exact reaction. Therefore, at the precise moment, flex your body like a rubber band that's been snapped.

In a woman-to-woman combat, you may be asked to pull your opponent's hair. In such cases, the person whose hair is being pulled controls the stunt. That person would place her hands atop the hand of the person *appearing* to pull her hair and move in the direction of the pull. Regardless of whose hair is being pulled – actor or stunt person – no one should feel a thing if skilled safety is practiced. I got to where I am by carefully following the tried and proven advice of people who have been in the business of stunts and stunt related performances long before me. I tried it and it worked for me as well, which is why and how I feel confident to share my stunt tips, advice and secrets for success with you. To that I would also like to add some great advice from a few friends who to me are legendary. Their tips are as follows:

Safety Tips and Advice for High Falls

Veteran stuntman Bob Brown – a high fall specialist, recognizes that the superstars of extreme sports have upped the ante in terms of the level to which stunt people must now rise to reach in terms of performing high falls. On his list of proudest accomplishments, Bob includes high falls at 150 feet and higher during which his technique includes somersaults and twists while making the fall seem visually and totally out of control. As both a performer and stunt coordinator, Bob confesses, "I would never ask anyone– including myself, to repeat a fall." In other words, as fun as this business may seem, it's called show-BUSINESS for a good reason.

Bob's inspiration comes from great high fall legends Ronnie Rondell, Terry Leonard, Bobby Bass and Dar Robinson, who blazed the trail before him. Bob is all too familiar with the additional pressure to perform live versus a pre-recorded performance that can be repeated over and over until perfection is achieved. He understands the difference between performing for television and film, all of which makes a difference great difference to the stunt performer.

"Professional is key," is Bob's belief. And I agree! "The best high fall stunt performers in the history of the business come with a background in trampoline gymnastics and high diving," is another one of Bob's beliefs. The sport of trampolining includes simple jumps in the pike, tuck or straddle positions, as well as the far more complicated combinations of forward and backward somersaults and twists. "The more of these specialties you combine, the better," he explains.

Safety Tips for Successful Driving

Along the way to becoming one of the best stunt drivers in the business, my friend and mentor Jalil Jay Lynch offers the following advice:

- First, and foremost, always respect the vehicle. Treat it as if it's a deadly weapon. Always be aware of your surroundings. Make sure the car you are driving has a seat belt. Keep in mind that every car is different. Get to know each car you drive.
- Next, choose a safe, desolate area. Check the air pressure of your tires. Allow more air for dry surface. A minimal air pressure of 15-20 pounds higher than the suggested air pressure will help the tires adhere to the rims and helps the car slide easier.
- Make sure the surface is level, as in free of potholes and dips so as not to overturn the car. Use cones to create a mark to slide to or stop-on. Create an environment to hone your skills versus a lot of sliding around aimlessly. Visualize, commit and then execute.

- A reputable driving school is an absolute must for the basics of driving and beyond. And Jim Wilkey of Bobby Ore Motorsports, is amongst the best in the business. He suggests:
- Thoroughly check and double check the vehicle's interior for unsecured items that could move around and run the risk of being positioned between your foot and the gas or brake pedals.
- Always look to your mark. In other words, have a focal point and keep your eyes on it. The mark on which your eyes are focused will usually determine where you go.
- Turn your head in the direction you want to take the car. For example, let's say you're performing a 180-degree turn. Once you've executed your lock up, meaning your rear wheels are no longer spinning, your head should be turned as far around as possible in the direction of your focal point.
- Keep your steering wheel movements to a minimum when performing maneuvers. Otherwise you may end up over steering, resulting in a sloppy, less than professional turn. Debbie Evans, another highly acclaimed Hollywood stuntwoman, started riding motorcycles at the age of six. She entered her first motorcycle trails competition at age nine, becoming a competitive expert shortly thereafter, against both male and female challengers. Debbie's Yamaha sponsorship paved the way for many halftime performances. During stadium events she would routinely wow the crowd with her signature headstand on the seat of a balancing motorcycle. Debbie's advice includes:
- Rule number one: Don't take a job unless you can do it.
- Don't over sell yourself. Be honest in what you can and can't do.

- It's important to train and be able to drive all kinds of cars and SUV's.
- Learn the unique driving characteristics of driving a stick shift versus an automatic transmission and front wheel drive versus rear and all wheel drive. Each has the ability to respond totally different under similar driving conditions.

Safety Tips for Successful Rigging

If you can master the techniques of rigging, chances are, you'll have a lasting career in this business and build a great reputation for yourself, which will help to grow you as an expert or a brand.

When it comes to the various types of rigging I turn to my friend, stunt coordinator Norbert Phillips. In addition to the work he does through his California-based company Got Rigging, Norbert also handled rigging and coordinated stunts for the hit television series *"Fear Factor."* His suggestions for safe rigging are as follows:

- Double inspect your harness to ensure there is no visible damage, including cuts in the webbing and rust on the buckles. If either is present, request a replacement. Make sure the harness is the right size for you: If you can close the harness all the way down with no space left to tighten, then it's too big for you.
- The biggest mistake people make when it comes to ratchets is not asking questions. As a performer, I want to know my final "psi," or pounds per square inch. Every ratchet is unique and each person has his own way of riding one. So always try to build up to a final psi and make sure that you hear what it is. Know your angles. A 28-degree angle at 450 psi is a flat-fast ratchet, while a 45-degree

angle at 225 psi is a flat-soft ride. Make sure the operator confirms your pressure before you ride a ratchet. Don't budge until you get a confirmation, such as, for example, "We're hot at 450psi." Then, this should be followed by action from the stunt person.

- Perhaps the best safety tip concerning an air ram (a pneumatic device that catapults a stunt performer through the air) is to never put your face by the device. Theoretically, the air ram is a loaded gun. If you touch the air ram, it will fire. Therefore, always assume it's "hot" and approach with caution. As with the ratchet, know your pressure and hear it called out before you ride. And like a ratchet, every air ram is uniquely determined by bore size, cylinoid size and bottle size. Just because the last ram you rode may have been smooth at 150 psi, don't freak out if you're told the pressure of the next ride is 500 psi. That just means it takes more pressure to move the ram and your weight.

Safety Tips for Stunts Involving Fire

Stuntman and fellow World Taurus Stunt Award recipient Eddie Fernandez offers the following "Tuesday's Tips" at www.iStunt.com:

- Get plenty of rest the night before. This will help your focus the following day.
- Communication on the set. Everyone should be on the same page. Be alert – focus, pay attention and communicate.
- Never panic. It will just bring confusion to the set. It also ruins communication, leading to physical harm to yourself and (possible) danger to the crew.

- Usually, when using a fire extinguisher, it's because you're doing a medium to full burn, which means the time frame to douse someone is very important. Once the person on fire is ready to be extinguished, he or she should lie on the ground like a cross, if possible. The first safety person should have a damp towel to place over the stunt person's head. This will do three things: 1) protect face from flames, 2) allow for breathing, and 3) provide protection from inhaling chemicals that may be spread by the fire extinguisher. With that said, if a person inhales an extinguisher's chemicals, it could cause damage to the lungs. So, the towel is crucial. Moreover, if the stunt is done outdoors where the wind might be a factor, be mindful that the wind may blow chemicals back into your face, which brings me to the second safety person: the extinguisher. The person dousing the flames should be directly behind the individual with the towel, then spraying at a 45-degree angle from shoulder to toe. This will avoid breathing chemicals that may boomerang into the face. The third, and final, safety person should have a fire damp blanket to smother the fire if the blaze has not been fully extinguished. Working with is fire akin to a dance – a person's move needs be smooth and precise.
- When do you know it's it time to be extinguished from a fire burn? That should be determined between the person being set on fire and the fire coordinator. An average burn should be from 10 to 20 seconds
- If you're not comfortable with a certain stunt, make sure you say something to your coordinator. As always, safety is first. To Eddie's tips I would also insist that you double-check your equipment. If I'm unsure about the security of my harness or

whether I've slathered on enough fire-retardant gel, I am very quick to speak up and let someone know. After all, it's not only my life, but also the lives of others who could be on the line each time a stunt is performed. Keep that in mind so that each time you perform a stunt you are prepared to give the best performance possible. Study and ask questions for a good understanding of every stunt you're considering.

And always, always, always continue to train in your area of specialty, and in general.

CHAPTER 7

BUILDING YOUR BRAND

(Photo Credit:
Shawn Barber)

❧ ❯ ❧

People think opportunity knocks. I had to go out to find it, sometimes create it and then bring it home. That's marketing. It's an essential element to your success in the stunt business.

Here's what works for me:

A. Having good photos

- Have a good 3/4 body shot. Several important elements are considered when a stunt double is cast. These include height, weight, physique, hair color, bone structure, etc. Present a good body shot so the coordinator can decide if you are a believable double for the actor.
- Wear clothing that's suitable to your body type, but nothing too revealing. For girls, it could be a tank top, yoga pants or a halter and jeans. For guys, a tank top and jeans are cool. This helps the stunt coordinator see what you really look like, especially if he or she has never met you before.

- Always look like your photo. If you send in a picture of yourself as a size-4 with red hair, you better show up as a size-4 with red hair. If not, chances are the stunt coordinator may not hire you. Worse, the stunt coordinator may not ever consider you *again* because he or she doesn't know what version of you is going to walk through the door. It's a trust factor. Speaking of which, I hear that some coordinators are now requesting photos be shot and sent on the spot via cell phone since it's no longer uncommon to show up looking very different from previously submitted head shot.
- Include action shots. These include photos performing gymnastics, martial arts, surfing, etc. After all, it's a stunt job you're after. So, show yourself doing stunts.
- An online search will identify photographers in your area. Also, ask around for personal referrals.
- Make sure photographers are legitimate. Ask for references and review their portfolios.
- During the first meeting with a photographer, evaluate the synergy between both of you.
- Examine the photographer's work, and details including lighting. Did you see pictures in his portfolio of others with similar complexion to yours? Was the make-up natural or glamorous? The more natural you appear in pictures, the easier it is for hair and make-up on the set to envision your final look.
- Most professional photographers charge $300 and up, excluding hair and makeup. At that price, your package may include one 8x10 retouched photo, with the remaining images on a CD. At the $700 level, the package may include three retouched 8x10 photos, with all others from the shoot on a CD. These are ballpark figures based on my experiences. Just remember, you get what you pay for. For a $50 shoot, you'll likely get $50 quality work.

- Makeup could run an additional $100 and up, as could hair. Check around.
- Be sure to ask the photographer about price specials.

B. Having good résumé(s)

You definitely want to look your best on paper and be able to back it up in person. I use multiple résumés to highlight my stunt expertise. Case in point, I have one résumé for all my stunt work, in general, that I've done in film and television. But when a production company is considering me for a precision-driving stunt, I submit a separate résumé listing only previous driving gigs. When creating your résumé remember to ...

- Include the name of the film, television series or show, and the stunt coordinator or director with whom you worked. Remember everyone is connected in this business. So in this case, it's OK to name-drop.
- List your commercial work in a separate section. When you do here's something to keep in mind: Say, for example, you're auditioning for a Toyota commercial. However, your résumé lists work you've done on a Ford commercial that catches the attention of the people casting for Toyota. Chances are there will be some concern about your association with both brands – especially if the commercials end up running at the same time, which is not allowed. To avoid the possibility of any potential conflict that could disqualify you for the job, you might want to structure the commercial section of your résumé as follows:
- List only the commercial stunt(s) you've performed, the name of the coordinator and the words "Commercial list provided upon request."

- If the Ford commercial is still running, chances are Toyota is not going to hire you. If it's not, at least you will have the opportunity to explain before being rejected.
- List special skills such as martial arts, driving, gymnastics, scuba diving, expert swimming, stage combat, archery, firearms, rappelling, ratchets, free running and football.
- List special licenses, including motorcycle, forklift operator, truck or boat. Since few people have these, you're likely to stand out.
- List every performance you've ever done (union, non-union or an independent film). Be sure to update your résumé regularly.
- Recently, I read in the Hollywood Reporter how A-list actors are in search of juicier roles by way of indie-film projects. According to the Hollywood Reporter, "With fewer studio films being produced, known actors are much more willing to look at indie-scripts to keep working and to find meatier roles, money be damned. Actors with mainstream careers – Halle Berry, Kirsten Dunst, Elizabeth Banks and more – are eagerly digging back into indie-fare." In your efforts to break into the business, I highly suggest you pursue indie-film projects, short films and student films to help build your credits. For a better sense of what a good résumé looks like, visit www.angelameryl.com. Most importantly, choose what works best for you.

C. POSTCARDS

Postcards are an inexpensive and efficient marketing resource.

On the front of your postcard, consider using an action shot and/or headshot – something that's going to grab attention. On the back, put a smaller photo along with a short phrase. For instance, "I just worked on the film _____," or "I just got my black belt in karate," or simply, "Just wanted to say hello." Be sure to include your contact information. The last thing you want is to have a great postcard with no way for people to get in touch with you. But, do not include home phone numbers.

Postcards are most effective because:

- At a glance, a coordinator can see who you are and any pertinent information
- With no envelope to open, it assures your message will be viewed instantly Whatever you write, keep it short and sweet. You're dealing with busy professionals. But, they're not too busy to glance at a postcard. I can't tell you how many times I've gone to a production set to introduce myself to stunt coordinators, or run into one I already know, only to hear, "Oh yeah, I got your postcard."

(Photo Credit: Russel baer)   Training with Marcus Salgado

D. Business Cards

Business cards with your picture, contact info and Web site address are the next best thing to postcards. In fact, they may be the least expensive way to advertise. Always keep some in your wallet. When out to dinner or at a party you can easily pass along a business card, which you could never do as casually with a headshot. Never leave home without them.

Keep a supply of business cards in your car at all times. Sometimes you'll go on a set thinking there's only one stunt coordinator when there may actually be several. For that reason, keep available headshots with your résumé attached, postcards, a stapler, sticky notes (in case you want to leave a note along with your headshot), a marker or pen, some 8x11 envelopes and additional copies of your reel in your car, as well. Remember, promoting you is a full-time job.

E. Your Reel

A reel is video footage of work you've done. It's you in action.

Keep your reel to 1 minute and no more than 1 1/2 minutes, especially if it accompanies a headshot and other marketing materials. Stay true to your objective. On average, coordinators don't have the time or interest to view a 5-minute reel. Save that one for your Web site. For your submission, keep it simple. A well-edited minute of footage should demonstrate your best efforts. A few actionpacked clips should illustrate you doing what you say you can do, whether from actual work or from choreographed routines with friends. This will help get you hired. If you are an experienced fighter, you can get together with friends and shoot a mini-fight sequence. This bears repeating: Remember to check your distance and maintain eye contact at all times for safety's sake. Put together a really simple sequence with a few punches and kicks, maybe a couple of flips – and the next thing you know, you've got a believable fight scene.

Even if it's just you doing gymnastics, have someone shoot it, upload it on YouTube and then attach the link to your Web site. We've all seen people achieve "overnight success" by uploading footage once dismissed as silly video but eventually aired on *"The Today Show"* or *"The Tonight Show,"* bringing instant fame. If you get enough hits, this could be you.

F. Your Web site

Now that we've discussed the benefits of having a reel, pictures and other basic marketing tools, it's time to bring them all together on a Web site.

If you have the time and patience, save yourself some money by creating your own online presence through a Web-hosting service such as Word Press or GoDaddy. Their software makes the entire process simple. And with today's content management systems, updating a Web site – which, in the past, could only be done through a costly programmer – is now as simple as creating or editing a document in Microsoft Word.

Your homepage should show you in action. My suggestions are as follows:

The moment visitors land on your site, captivate them with a really great body shot and your action-packed reel. Remember, people have very short attention spans, which means you've got to put your best foot forward immediately.

- Avoid using excessive graphics on your homepage so as not to confuse or slow down visitors to your site.
- Make the site extremely easy to navigate.

- Post your résumé with contact information, excluding your home number. Listing the number of a local stunt answering service is one option here.
- Include any articles written about you, even from your neighborhood newspaper. Someone from the newspaper thought you were interesting. Why wouldn't someone else?
- Create an e-mail addresses with your Web site domain as a means for others to get in touch with you, and take note of your brand through your Web site address. Create separate e-mail addresses for personal mail, media inquiries and general inquiries.

If you don't have the time or the patience, turn it over to an expert Web site developer for $200 and up. You'll have online presence in no time.

G. Social Media

Social media is a marketing tool, where the content you create is designed to attract attention and encourage readers to share throughout their social networks. If you don't already have a Facebook page, Twitter account, YouTube account, or LinkedIn profile, you should seriously consider having one or all. Here's why ...

Facebook: Practically the whole world is on Facebook – even celebrities. It's the online version of text messaging with pictures and video all in one. I've been hired because of a stunt coordinator's visit to my page. I would highly recommend that you have a presence on Facebook. You need to be found. And in the big- profile business of entertainment, people need to find you with ease.

Twitter: When you're working Twitter is a great way to share the excitement right from your phone. Let people you follow and people who follow you know the stunts you're performing that day. Excite them by sharing the process, especially when you're doubling a celebrity. Case in point: While doubling Rihanna in the movie *"Battleship,"* my tweets were all the rage when I shared with followers that, playfully, she grabbed my left boob and welcomed me in as a member of the crew.

YouTube: As the largest worldwide video-sharing community, YouTube is an excellent venue for showcasing your reel.

LinkedIn: Unlike the other social media outlets where it's OK to be playful, LinkedIn is for the more serious-minded professional looking to network. Listings flow by name and profession, and there is a stunt listing. With the use of social media, you can now see how easy it is to make your presence known throughout the world.

H. Agents

For television commercials you really want to have an agent.

Agents receive daily lists of upcoming commercials called "breakdowns." They give a pretty thorough description of the types of commercial actors to be cast and the specific need for stunts.

Commercials can be very lucrative. For example, if you're acting in a commercial, you'll get paid scale – a term that defines the union standard for wages. If you're acting and performing a stunt in a commercial, you may qualify for a payment adjustment in addition to scale. Cha-ching! Then there's the whole matter of residuals or additional compensation for the reuse of your work. In other words, each time the commercial airs, you'll get paid as long as it's not a buyout, meaning a flat rate for your performance. For me, buyouts have ranged in the area of $1,000 to $2,500 per commercial, which ain't bad for a day's work. If commercials are the direction in which you'd like to go, start watching to see if there's someone in television ads who looks like you. A casting director once told me, "If you see someone who looks like you in a commercial, chances are there is work for you." If you don't see yourself in commercials, you may have to create your own path until you're discovered. By that I mean marketing yourself, or "hustling," which I'll further explain in the following chapter later. These include mailing, e-mailing and faxing headshots and résumés, as well as sending reel to stunt coordinators. To help you create a list of agents to target, my suggestion is that you read the "Call Sheet Book" to identify commercial agents specializing in stunts and sports. Then send out headshots and résumés, respectively. Some agents accept clients only by referral. Carefully read the description for a clear understanding before contacting potential agents. See the resource guide for where to find the "Call Sheet Book."

The best way to get work and keep working in the stunt business is by developing and maintaining good relationships with stunt coordinators. Agents are helpful when you're going after stunt work in television commercials, and in film – when the role requires extensive dialogue. Still, in large part, your relationships with stunt coordinators will really make the difference when it comes down to booking the job. By that, I mean anyone could be cast for a commercial stunt; however, in the end, it is the stunt coordinator who will have the final say.

O. Hangouts and training spots

In areas where you live, work and play, it's important that you identify with other stunt people. This will help you develop a base of friends who do what you do and make it easier to access information relative to your career. For example, business people commonly meet at happy hour or on the golf course to exchange ideas and make deals. For you, my suggestion is to find out where other stunt people train and hang out in their leisure time so that you can stay up on what's hot and what's not in the stunt business.

Here's how it worked for me: When I started out in New York as a driver in the movie *"Dead Presidents,"* the first assistant director on the set referred me to the stunt coordinator on the set of *"New York Undercover."* One of the stunt guys I worked with on *"New York Undercover"* also worked on the HBO series *"Oz"* and referred me to the stunt coordinator there. That became my third gig. As soon as I moved to Los Angeles, my friend Brennan Dyson introduced me to Hjelte Sports Center in Encino, Calif. Hijelte is where stunt people from all over southern California gather on weekends to have a great time over a good game of softball. The league forms every year in January, organized by stuntman and stunt coordinator Larry Rosenthal. Larry is always in search of good players.

If interested, contact him via email at larrystunts@yahoo.com.

Also in the Los Angeles area, Valley College is another great place to meet like-minded people. For about $5 on Tuesdays and Fridays, you can park for free and meet people practicing at a gymnasium laden with mats, balance beams, trampolines and more. It's where I met Eric Betts – one of the original Power Rangers. Eric then became my very first fight trainer for film and television.

Businesses that offer training and other stunt-specific events oftentimes use a stunt service to help spread the word. Always try to attend those that you hear about. It's a great way to meet others in the business.

Over the years I've come across lots of information and helpful tips through Bill's Stunt Service and Missy's Action Services in Los Angeles, all of which have worked together to help further my career.

Stunt groups are known to sponsor or register for events that benefit them. Some of the most popular events include

The Troy Melton Memorial Golf Tournament, SWAMP's (Stuntwomen's Association of Motion Pictures) Annual Bowling Tournament and my all-time favorite, Day In The Dirt. This three-day action-packed motorcross grand prix event draws stunt people from coast to coast. Groups such as V10 (to which I belong) all have booths with promo items for sale and stunt people everywhere. The Stock Car Racing Series at Speedway Willow Springs, one of the eight tracks at the Willow Springs International Raceway in Rosamond, California, is another popular attraction. A lot of the drivers come directly from Rick Seaman's Motion Picture Driving Clinic. You'll probably meet Rick there, too. If you don't live in Los Angeles, get creative by discovering what's in your own back yard based on the examples I've shared. You should also consider attending some of the events listed above. Again, the more people you know, the more opportunities you will have to advance your career. Mary Albee, a renowned stunt coordinator, once said to me, "If you're not putting in at least 40-hours a week to get into this business and stay, then you're not taking it seriously and I suggest you go out and get a job."

CHAPTER 8

THE SETUP TO GET YOU WORKING

(Photo Credit:
Shawn Barber)

❦ ⟩ ❦

Having shared so many of the tried-and-true practices that have brought me where I am in my career today, now is as good a time as ever to tell you what I do and where I go to find work.

Stunt service

A stunt service is a phone service used by stunt people and stunt coordinators. It's an easy way for a stunt coordinator to get in contact with you simply by calling the service and asking for you. The service will either connect the coordinator directly to you or call you with a message from the coordinator.

The service is helpful and efficient for coordinators who can make one or two calls and hire multiple people. A coordinator may sometimes call a stunt service and say, "I need someone 5 feet, 5 inches tall, weighing 125 pounds, with black hair. Who do you have?" The service will search its database to match the criteria. Therefore, it is important to keep your information current to avoid the potential loss of work.

Services start at approximately $50 monthly and may include additional fees for call- forwarding, excessive calls or the use of their number. My recommendation is that you belong to more than one stunt service. You'll be found faster and easier by coordinators. SAG membership is required, and in some cases you have to be referred by a stunt person, or coordinator.

Stunt Contact and Production Weekly

"The Stunt Contact" and *"Production Weekly"* are excellent resources for upcoming productions and those currently in pre-production or shooting. They list the identity of the coordinator and the location of the production office, which is where you can send a headshot, résumé and reel for consideration. Some productions companies have even gone green, whereby providing e-mail addresses for submissions versus mail-ins. Actors are often included in the listing. If you believe you would make a good double for any actor listed, then, by all means, go to the set and drop off (or e-mail) your headshot, résumé and reel to the coordinator. Be sure to include a brief cover letter of introduction. If the coordinator is with a stunt group, drop off your picture, résumé and reel at the group's office – if they have one. Otherwise you may have to send the information electronically. In the next section I'll tell you more about stunt groups.

Stunt Directories

Just like there are phone directories, there are stunt directories. To a business, being listed in a phone directory – whether in print or online – is an essential to draw customers. It's like the road that leads the customer to the business.

Stunt directories are similar. They lead stunt coordinators to stunt people.

Let me break it down to you like this: It's far more difficult to become a member of a stunt group mainly because of the number of years of experience most stunt groups require. While stunt groups are mainly interested in more seasoned and experienced stunt people, the qualifications for a listing in a stunt directory tend to be a bit less stringent.

Case in point, I was doing stunts in New York about four years and an additional two years after I arrived in Los Angeles when one of the members of the V10 Stunt Group approached me with an invitation to join. She had already done her homework by asking stunt coordinators about me and decided I'd probably be a good fit for the group. At that time, I had already purchased a listing in The Stunt Players Directory, which was the only stunt directory until about 2010.

Truth be told, I had never thought about being in a stunt group. I just wanted to work consistently in the business. Becoming a member of V10, however, gave me a further sense of belonging in the business, similar to what it probably feels like to be a member of a sorority or fraternity. Was it necessary? No. But helpful? Yes.

The bottom line is that it's definitely harder to get into a stunt group than it is to get listed in a stunt directory. Both will lead to work, just at different levels. For example, if you're just getting in the business, you should definitely be listed in as many stunt directories as possible. It's a great way to be seen by a multitude of stunt coordinators. Once you've been in the game and are well-seasoned, your membership in a stunt group says just that. It provides coordinators with a greater level of comfort in terms of what you're capable of pulling off. For example, I was able to get work doubling Vanessa Williams during my first four years in the business, which is pretty good. After I became a member of V10, I started getting calls that led me to doubling other top names in Hollywood such as Halle Berry, Beyoncé, Vivica A. Fox, Gabrielle Union, Rihanna and others. The business of stunt directories all began with The Stunt Players Directory. Since then, newcomers – up until the time I wrote this book – include "*The Stunt Phone Book*" and "*iStunt*."

For your convenience, each one is listed in the resource guide at the end of this book.

"Hustling" a Stunt Coordinator

Being new to Los Angeles, I had to go out and approach coordinators in an effort to introduce myself. We call this hustling. Then, there's the referral. A referral is when someone you already know has a connection with a coordinator you'd like to meet and is willing to introduce you. To hustle, or meet and greet coordinators, you need to know where the productions are shooting. For me, that meant first studying the stunt directory and trade publications. Then, while driving around Los Angeles, I would stop my car and ask what was being shot whenever I saw what appeared to be a production. Once I knew the title, I could cross-reference my stunt directory and the trades to see if the production was reported to have stunts. If it did, I would park my car and try to slip by security at base camp. Base camp is the area where hair, makeup, wardrobe (sometimes all referred to as the honeywagon – when in one unit) and production office trailers are usually stationed. I'd enter the production office and leave my picture and résumé for the coordinator. I would also try to discover the location of the set either by asking the PA (production assistant) or anyone who looks like they might know. Otherwise, I'd go snooping around for some type of lead, such as a number of equipment trucks. From there I'd simply follow the trail to the set. Once on the set, I'd try to locate and make contact with the coordinator.

Most times I went alone so as not to draw too much attention. Oftentimes a woman can get by a production assistant much easier than a man. Act like you belong there and chances are they won't stop you. This is a hard business to crack, and confidence counts.

When you meet a coordinator keep it brief. Tell them a few things about yourself including your recent projects. If you haven't worked recently, be sure to tell them what you're capable of doing. Perhaps the best advice I can give you is to listen to what the coordinator has to say. He or she may give you the exact information you need. But you've got to know when to shut up and listen. If the coordinator is busy and you stick around and become a nuisance, your résumé will likely become a trash can liner. Even though you may have left your résumé, photo and reel at the production office, put it in the coordinator's hand if you meet him or her. Then be on your way. Should you stay, do so only if the coordinator asks you. Remember they're working.

Keep in mind set etiquette. In other words, if lunch is being served and you're not invited, don't wait around looking desperate or pitiful to gain a free meal or get hired. If you're asked to remain on the set, sit or stand where you're told. But never sit in the chair of a cast member or director – since you're not there to work.

Avoid embarrassment: For example, a newcomer to the stunt community arrives on the set and attempts to locate the stunt crew. As she comes across a would-be group of people whose looks fit the profile, she asks for the stunt coordinator by name. Unbeknownst to her, she was actually speaking to the coordinator, who purposely clowns her by identifying himself as someone else. Because of ignorance, the joke was on the newcomer for not doing her homework. The moral of the story is that she failed to research the stunt coordinator in any of the available resource guides (IMDB, Stunt Players Directory, etc.). Even as a last-minute resort, she should have sought the help of a production assistant on the set to help identify the coordinator. Please, don't let that be you.

Casting Services Online

At Actors Access, you can register free online and create a profile that will be entered into the Breakdown Services database, which is regularly searched by casting directors seeking specific talent. When creating a profile specify your areas of expertise so that the optional e-mail notification service can alert you to a role that matches your talent criteria.

Actors Access is great for everyone from beginners to the more seasoned stunt performer. Beginners are likely to find student film projects shooting locally on the weekends and short films with light stunts.

You can also view the daily Breakdown for roles posted by casting directors for film, television and commercials. Should you choose to submit yourself for a posted role, a $2 processing charge will apply for each submission. By subscribing to Showfax for $68 a year, you'll have unlimited privileges for electronic submissions.

Both Actors Access and Showfax are divisions of Breakdown Services Ltd. Altogether they service markets throughout the U.S. and in Canada, on both the talent and casting sides.

Casting Networks is a totally separate organization that does the same thing as Actors Access.

The Trade Publications

Because of tax incentives made available to filmmakers, not all the action is in Los Angeles or New York these days. Films are being shot in Louisiana, New Mexico, Georgia, Michigan, Florida and other states. Keep an eye on trade magazines for productions coming to your area. *Variety* and *The Hollywood Reporter* once published lists each week. Now it's just *The Hollywood Reporter* on Tuesdays. *Backstage* also publishes a list online every Thursday. It's very important to keep in mind that the location of your SAG membership is the area where you're considered a local hire. For most union gigs, SAG by-laws typically require a local hire based on the specific description of the stunt and the specialty of the stunt person. This is why it's important that you take the work you do seriously and be the best you can be.

See the resource guide at the end of this book for a list of trade publications where you will find other production listings.

CHAPTER 9

GET THE JOB: THIS ONE, THAT ONE AND
THE NEXT ONE, TOO

(Photo Credit: Shawn Barber)

~≈ >≈~

You never know what stunt you may be asked to perform. So, if your goal is to stay employed in this business, I can't stress how important it is for you to be well-rounded.

Aside from stunt and stunt-related training, consider taking classes to increase your acting and improvisation skills. Since a stunt person must act like something is happening or pretend to be someone, acting classes will help make your performance more believable.

Allow me to share some personal experiences where I had to learn on the job or take a crash course to keep working in this business...

I was once called to do a scuba diving job. Without any certification or skills in diving, I had no choice but to be honest with the stunt coordinator during the call. When he asked if I could scuba dive, I told him I could not. In the same breath I asked him how much time I had to get up to speed. He said there was roughly a month before the shoot was scheduled. I called around to a few places, found a scuba diving course and took the plunge. Two weeks later,

I was a licensed scuba diver and ready to double Beyoncé in *"Austin Powers in Goldmember."*

With a new skill in my hip pocket I climbed into a Mini Cooper and sat next to Andy Gill – the stunt double for Mike Meyers. We buckled our seat belts and waited for the director to yell "Action!" Then, Andy drove into the polluted seaport waters of the San Pedro (California) Bay, where the car filled slowly with water.

In the film, Mike Meyers wore glasses, which allowed the props people to come up with a mask for Andy. Because Beyoncé's character had nothing on her face, I could not wear a mask or place the mini regulator in my mouth until the water was nearly over my head, otherwise the cameras would see it. Without a mask I kept my eyes shut and pinched my nose with one hand, while holding the regulator in the other. Once fully submerged and out of the camera's view, I placed the regulator in my mouth in order to breathe under water. I gave an occasional nod to the safety divers to signify that I was OK. We sat submerged in the water around 30 seconds, which seemed like a lifetime. Then they pulled the car out of the water and yelled, "Cut! Back to one," which meant we had to do it all over again. Have you ever been trapped in a car while it fills slowly, and completely, with water so murky that you can barely see in front of you? If not, let me tell you. That's a very frightening experience. Through it all, I had to keep reminding myself: *"You can swim. You can hold your breath. Air is coming soon."* That really helped me to stay focused. In another situation the casting director at a television commercial audition wanted each stunt person to show up at the casting office with a mountain bike. After signing in, we had to go outside one by one, ride down a hill and perform a "90," while sliding toward the camera. (For the record, a "90" is actually a 45-degree angle turn in the stunt world.) When I did my "90" I put way too much pressure on the front brakes. I flipped over the handlebars, hit the ground, then jumped up and said, "*Ta-da!*" It was as if I'd done the whole thing on purpose. There had to be at least 10 other people watching from the hallway window of the casting office when the assistant casting director/camera operator yelled out, "Ohmigod! Are you OK?"

"I'm all right," I said.

Once he was certain that I was all right, we both laughed hysterically. Then he said, "Okay, let's do that again." And I said, "Do WHAT," which made us laugh all over again. In the end, I booked the job, thanks to quick thinking and a good attitude.

Early in my career, while working on the set of "*The Time Machine*," I was asked to do a ratchet. A ratchet is a process where a vest-like harness is worn beneath undergarments and connected via cable at various pick points on the harness. It allows you to be pulled in an instant from a compelling scene, such as an explosion. Seeing it in action probably will remind you of a scene from a Peter Pan movie, with stunt people flying through the air. But, in reality, there is no guarantee that the stunt person will have a soft landing. Naturally, when I was asked to do my first ratchet I was a little nervous because I had never done one before. Stunt coordinator Bob Brown stood next to me, just outside of frame.

"I'll walk you through it: Just remember to tuck your chin into your chest, and then you're just a passenger going for a ride on a wire," he said. Then Bob told me to lean forward so that the cable rigged to the harness would remain taunt. "Action," the director yelled.

The rig was activated and, in an instant, I flew backwards, smack dab into the pile of pads that were there to keep my head from smashing into the ground. Bob had faith in me, and I trusted him.

Knowing the potential for injury in this business, I make it a policy to accept work only that I'm pretty sure I can do. I deviate from that policy only if the coordinator says, "I really think you can do this." The reason is that coordinator may think I have a wider range of skills than I realize. Having worked with me in the past, he may feel assured that what I'm being asked to do is not too much of a stretch based on my past experiences and capabilities. Believe in yourself. That is the best advice I can offer. Then too, trust the coordinator's judgment. He is far more seasoned in this business.

CHAPTER 10

(Photo Credit:
Shawn Barber)

PREPARATION BEYOND SKILLS

⇜ ❭❦⇝

There will come days when out of the clear blue sky you may be asked to audition. To pull it off, you've got to look the part, be the part and do the stunt to perfection if you want to work again.

When I doubled Halle Berry in *"Their Eyes Were Watching God,"* I showed up on the set in tight jeans and a fitted shirt. That was my interpretation of Halle. I was asked to stand at a distance while she checked me out, but not to look at her in the process. After she approved of me, I was off to hair and makeup. That audition was pretty easy. There were many other times in my career, however, when an entire team has had to weigh in before final approval was given. After being selected by the stunt coordinator, the approval team included the A-list celebrity and her hair and makeup people.

So that you are prepared at any given time, keep your stunt gear and a change of clothes in your car. A sexy pair of jeans, a T-shirt that would bear your arms, and boots with heels work for me. Guys, you might want to have a pair of jeans and a tank top or T-shirt. I keep it sexy and simple with each of these items in my stunt bag so that I am always ready, willing and able to audition for work. Find a look that works for you and do the same.

My stunt gear bag includes:
Mouth piece
Elbow pads (hard and soft)
Forearm pads
Gator back pads (in both full and half sizes)
Kidney pads (hard and soft)
Hip Pads (hard and soft)
Tail-bone pads (hard and soft)
Thigh pads
Girdle (to conceal your pads); Spanx for women; biker shorts for men
Knee pads (hard and soft)
Shin guards (hard and soft)
Rappelling gloves
Safety goggles
Ace bandage
Sports tape
New Skin

Moleskin
Harness
Nomex Fire Gear
Gel inserts (for shoes)
Lifts (can be purchased from a shoe maker, or visit www. shoelift.com)
Hand warmers and foot warmers
Wipes for personal cleanup
Extra feminine products for women
Extra bra and panties for women; men should have jockstrap and cup
Advil or what works for you.
An extra pen (to fill out contract or any other paper work)

Veteran stunt drivers Harry Wowchuk and Jim Wilkey suggest including the following items in your stunt bag:

Mini flashlight and extra batteries
Matchbox or hot wheels type Cars and chalk in case the stunt coordinator forgets his set.
Lap belt with appropriate hardware for I-bolts
A Life hammer seat belt cutter to cut the seat belt or hammer through a window in cases of emergency
A Leatherman, mini tool set which is the size of a sun glass case.
An accurate tire gage
A small pair of vice grips pliers for parking brake t-handle to keep parking brake in release mode
Gaffers tape to wrap around t-handle to keep parking brake in release mode
Mini tube cutter device for parking brake t-handle to keep in release mode
Needle nose pliers to pull ABS fuses ....normally has to be disconnected to get tires to lock up
Parking brake cable shortners (tools to tighten brake cables)
A Sharp knife
Roll of electrical tape

Self taping screws
Always take a walk around your car and inspect it for any loose items gas cap, spare tire lug nuts, battery is it —tied down, check fluids, head lights, check tire pressure.

Colleagues tell me that ice skating pads – for elbows, buttocks and knees – are the bomb. At $25 for one elbow pad, versus most other pads that typically run about the same price for a package of two, some might say ice skating pads are also very expensive. Speaking of pads, I'd also suggest you keep an extra set in case you need to share with the actor you're doubling.

If the stunt involves breaking glass (or broken glass) such as it did for me in a scene on the set of the television series, "24" – where glass windows exploded 8 feet above our heads, a liquid product called New Skin is one of my little tricks for protecting the skin. This liquid bandage goes on wet and forms a flexible, clear, antiseptic coating over the skin. Another product used to protect the skin is Moleskin. This flesh-colored adhesive cloth comes in larger size bands that can be cut out for a custom fit. It can even be used to protect your skin from the friction of a harness. It may be possible to even combine New Skin and Moleskin if the stunt is that intense.

In one instance, just before we heard the word "Action," the coordinator yelled: "Don't put your hands down first, or you'll get cut." The combination of common sense and experience told me to fall knees first, then hip, elbow and shoulders – most of which were padded. From knowing how to fall, wearing pads, using New Skin and applying common sense, I didn't get cut. Others weren't as fortunate. Some even left the set with blood dripping from their hands and elbows.

Also listed above and still worthy of mention are products made with Nomex. Thermal protecting Nomex is a friend to firemen, race car drivers, stunt people and anyone else who faces the possibility of coming in close contact with open flames. If I'm doing a stunt that involves fire, you can best believe I'm wearing Nomex undergarments. You can get them at a stunt specialty store such as Amspec in Los Angeles. You can also order online.

CHAPTER 11

SHOW ME THE MONEY

(Photo Credit:
Shawn Barber)

❦ ❭ ❦

The pay scale in this business, which you often will hear referred to as "scale," can vary according to film, television, or commercial performances. Each union, be it AFTRA (American Federation of Television and Radio Artists) or SAG (Screen Actors Guild) has its own scale.

At the time we went to print with this book, AFTRA was a performers' union representing a wide variety of talent including news, singers, recording artists, promo and voice-over announcers and other performers in commercials, stunts and specialty acts. SAG was an American labor union representing principal performers in film and television and background performers worldwide. The two have since merged. In an earlier chapter we spoke about qualifying for membership in SAG, which includes health care and a credit union, both of which I use. AFTRA has similar benefits and is much easier to join. For most of my career, I have been a member of both, paying dues twice annually, based on the income I earn.

As of May 2011, AFTRA scale for stunts begins at $838 daily or $3,121 weekly with SAG at $809 daily and $3,015 weekly.

Scale can vary based on whether it's a low-budget, ultra-low budget or ultra-ultra low-budget production. From that point, there can also be a stunt adjustment added to scale.

In terms of stunt adjustments, it sorts of works like this: Stunt coordinators have a budget to work with on every production. If it fits into the budget, the stunt coordinator – at his or her discretion – will pay the stunt person an adjustment in addition to scale. Think of this as a bonus. The total amount you could receive is solely determined by the stunt coordinator and based on the stunt to be performed and the level of difficulty.

Working overtime, your pay scale can increase per hour. There can also be a per diem if you work out of town. If you're working locally, there could be an additional payment for mileage that is contingent on various factors. In fact, there are a ton of itemizations, all of which can be quite confusing to explain and are, therefore, best explained by your union. Refer to the Resource Guide in this book for union Web sites and further contact information.

Practically everything there is to know about the job you get hired to perform and the documentation that justifies receiving compensation is found either on the production "Call Sheet" or the Performers Production Time Report Exhibit G.

The Call Sheet

Usually the night before you are due to report for a job, the assistant director will call to confirm your call time on the set. He or she will also provide you with a copy of the call sheet. The call sheet lists such vital information as the production office phone and fax numbers, the names of the directors and producers associated with the production, the title of show and episode number, which is absolutely necessary for updating your IMDB page.

The sheet changes daily. Its various sections list what will be shot for the day including set location, scene numbers and their page numbers from the script, the cast and character names with their pick-up or report times, make up times and set ready times. Stand-ins, photo doubles, special instructions such as needed equipment, props or special effects are all listed. The advance schedule or what's scheduled to be shot the following day is often listed in the final section of the sheet. Flip the call sheet over to reveal a complete list of departments within the production company and the names of the employees. If you do not receive a call sheet, ask for one.

The Performers Production Time Report Exhibit G

Aside from keeping precise details of your time on the set, wrap times and everything in between, this document keeps track of your stunt adjustments. Such finite details include meal times.

As a SAG member, mealtime is required every six-hours. If for some reason it just can't happen, a meal penalty becomes due to you. That means a few extra dollars in your pocket for every meal delayed or missed entirely. The fee for delayed meals increases in 15-minute increments. Exhibit G documents the totals.

You should also sign-in on Exhibit G when going in for a fitting. Working on a show that requires a special costume or uniform means wardrobe will want to see you for measurements and a final fitting, all of which takes time for which you deserve to be paid. Look for the payment itemization on your check under "wardrobe fitting" or "fitting." If any particular adjustment does not appear by the time you sign out, chances are the job you were performing may have concluded, or "wrapped," before the coordinator had a chance to add it to the document. You may also want to make note of your times in case there could be a discrepancy down the line in your check. As a backup, some of my colleagues make a photocopy of the document with their smart phones. Kind of hard to dispute a picture!

To sample Exhibit G on the SAG website, visit www. sag.org. My suggestion is that you take a few minutes to become familiar with each. At some point, you'll be very glad you did.

You can really make a good living by performing stunts. I'm talking six figures, and above, if you really apply yourself. You have to be persistent, stay on top of your game and want it bad enough. You must be willing to eat and breathe stunts daily.

CHAPTER 12

STAY TRUE TO YOU

(Photo Credit:
Shawn Barber)

❦ ❭ ❦

About three years into my West Coast stunt career, an audition came my way for a national commercial that required me to bungee jump from 110 feet. With 10 feet being the equivalent to one story, 110 feet is 11-stories high.

Lord knows I had no business going out for that job. For one, I didn't want to jump off anything that high while attached to a simple cable. Second, like most African-Americans, the thought of Bungee jumping is not at the top of my bucket list.

Here's a little not-so-known fact about the origin of Bungee jumping. Interestingly, this modern-day sport traces its roots to the South Pacific.

According to Rachel Naba, a writer/researcher on the Yahoo Contributor Network, "There was once a woman on the Pentecost Island in the Vanuatu jungles who ran away from her husband, Tamale. Trying to escape, the wife hid in a tall tree. But Tamale saw her and climbed the tree after her. The woman jumped out of the tree and her husband followed. The woman had tied vines to her feet to break her fall; Tamale had not. While she survived, Tamale did not. Since then, the men in the village began the tradition of the land-dives as a proof of strength and as a reminder to women that they will never be tricked again.

The tradition continues today. Built by the men of the village, a tower is made of natural, indigenous materials. Platforms are included in the tower at different elevations to provide "diving boards" for jumpers. The ground is made soft and spongy, and vines are gathered. With the ceremony performed after the rainy season, the vines are full of water and very elastic to help break the diver's fall. As the man jumps, the vines stretch and his fall is broken. He is pulled upward as his head grazes the ground below.

This rite, commonly referred to as "land diving," Naghol or N'gol, is known by outsiders to be a fertility rite. As the diver's head grazes the soil below, the land is made fertile and assures a good yam harvest. The rite, however, has much deeper and important meaning. It is largely kept from the tourists who pay to see the ceremony. It is a tradition crucial to the cultural and spiritual life of those who participate. Because of the spiritual and cultural importance of the rite, the esoteric knowledge of the N'gol ceremony may never be known to the outside world. The sacred initiation ceremony has become not only a tourist attraction but has "evolved" into one of the most popular "extreme sports" of modern times. The villagers of Vanuatu dive for many cultural and spiritual reasons. In today's culture most people jump solely for the "adrenaline rush."

Instead of running from my fear of Bungee jumping, I ran toward it. Arriving at the casting office, a number of girls waited to audition. I began to think to myself, *"I'm not going to get this."* That was weird for me because those kinds of negative thoughts rarely, if ever, enter my mind. The casting director and stunt coordinator placed us in a line to see who had the best height, skin tone and size to match the actress. Even as I overheard them talking about me, I thought, *"No way are they going to pick me."* But in the end, it came down to just two of us – me and another woman. She and I could see them going back and forth about which one of us to book for the job. In the end, they picked both of us.

That experience happened way before the book and video of "*The Secret*" became popular. If you read it or watched it, you probably remember the lesson it teaches about the Law of Attraction. In other words, I had focused my thoughts on this job, and the job became a reality. I went home and prayed: "*Oh, Lord. What have I gotten myself into*?" The next day I headed to rehearsal under the assumption that we were going to begin with a 40-foot jump to warm-up. In my mind I chose 40 feet because it was the highest height from which I had ever jumped. When I arrived I saw a 10-foot airbag and a crane. Right then I was overcome with fear. I tried to fight it by saying to myself, "*You can do this Angela. You can do it, girl.*" Then the coordinator said, "OK, girls. We're starting at 110 feet. Who's first?"

I thought, "*What? Are you kidding me*, because *I sure as hell ain't going first!*" So I watched as the other stunt woman went ahead of me. The crane lifted her 11 stories. When she got up there she jumped. And I thought, "*Well, good for you.*"

Now, it was my turn. With my harness in place, the crew hooked the cable to me. Then, the crane began to lift me up. Looking around, I saw the entire San Fernando Valley and damn near the Pacific Ocean in Santa Monica. The crane operator asked, "Have you ever jumped from this height before?"

"*Hell, no!*" I wanted to shout. But, I responded with a simple "*no*" instead.

At the top, he opened the cage door and told me to "step to the edge, spread your arms out like a T and dive." Without any further thought, I did exactly what he said. To the edge I stepped. Then, I paused for just a split second. I needed to be reassured that 11 stories below an airbag was there to catch me in case anything failed. Then, I went for it. That first step over the edge took my breath away. I could feel myself plummeting through the air faster and faster with every millisecond that passed. At the same speed as I plummeted, the thought that ran through my minds was *"Ohmigod, please cable be there to snatch me back so that my face doesn't end up splattered across the airbag."* Before I could think further, I had reached the end of the rope and repeatedly bounced up and down before finally being lowered to the ground. That's just the clean version I'm willing to share. But just think about it for a second, and I'm sure you can figure out which words I may have left out and where.

The third time we jumped the traditional way – with a little ankle cuff – versus the harness in the previous jumps. They put the cuff on, and up we went.

"This time," the director said, "I want you to dive straight down, and when you get to the bottom flip over to your back. Once you stop bouncing, sit up and grab your ankles." Keeping in mind that there was an airbag beneath me, I dived, bounced and attempted to grab my ankles, which was extremely challenging from that position – all of which reminded me to do some sit-ups when I got home. Afterward, I was lowered to the ground and I heard, "Good job. Angela. Let's do it one more time. But this time we want you to look like you're really enjoying yourself. Lots of screaming and laughing is what we need from you," the director said.

I had no problem with the screaming. The laughing part would definitely be an act, because at that point I was definitely not enjoying myself. I didn't feel comfortable or at ease about falling with just a cuff around my ankle. On the way up, for what was supposed to be the last jump of the day, I got a queasy feeling in my gut. My intuition was telling me that I shouldn't be doing this. Because I was still pretty new to Los Angeles, the main question on my mind throughout this moment of intense pressure was whether being true to me would hinder my ability to get hired again by this particular stunt coordinator or any other coordinator in the business ever again. By the time we reached the top, I was no longer fearful of what the coordinator might say or do. Even more, it was very clear to me that I did not want to jump. Before the cage door opened, I said aloud, *"I don't want to do this."*

"This is a national commercial," the crane operator reminded me. "Are you sure," he said? "Yes," I said, asking him to take me back down. All the way down he gave his best shot at trying to talk me back into it. But, I was absolutely sure I did not want to jump again. When we reached the ground, the coordinator, client and the agency representatives all asked, "What's wrong?

Are you ok?"

I assured them I was fine. I asked to speak to the coordinator alone. I then apologized to him for not wanting to do the job. I even offered to help him find a replacement. But I was out of there.

That was one of the hardest things that I've ever had to do in this business. To this day, I'm thankful that I was able to walk away and not feel pressured to stay simply because I really needed the money.

Later that evening I cried like a baby. I was scared that no one would hire me again. I called a mentor, who assured me that by following my gut instinct I had done the right thing. Even so, I moped around for a day or two in an emotional stoop. I soon got over it, dusted off and started looking for work all over again. As a matter of fact, not long afterward, I booked *"Kill Bill,"* for which I received nominations for Taurus World Stunt Awards in the categories of Best Overall Stunt by a Woman (for crashing through a glass coffee table) and Best Fight.

All in all the experience taught me to stay true to myself and not allow anyone to push me into something I don't want to do. And by the way, I'm still getting calls for work from that same stunt coordinator.

Part Three: Moving Forward

(Photo Credit: Shawn Barber)

CHAPTER 13

STILL TO COME

(Photo Credit:
Shawn Barber)

❧ ❭ ❧

W hen I got into this business the goals that mattered most to me were to do stunts as a full-time career without the need for a second job. That meant lining up job after job to live without the stress of not having enough money to support myself. I also wanted to live in a house in a nice neighborhood with a reliable car in the driveway or garage. I wanted to double leading ladies such as Halle Berry, Beyoncé and Vanessa L. Williams. I wanted to work with leading men, including Jamie Foxx, Robert De Niro and Samuel L. Jackson. I wanted to do a really brutal, kick-ass girl fight and come crashing through a sliding glass door. Fortunately, I've achieved every goal listed here and more.

Back when my career began there weren't nearly as many independent directors and producers creating projects and taking them to market at film festivals. Nowadays it's a common practice. In the process, stunt performers are coming up with jobs inside the business to stay connected to their dream. So you've got many of the younger players now landing coordinating jobs. They get them by shooting dynamic stunts scenes for presentation to directors and producers. By having actually coordinated the stunt they're now in a position to advise and consult with the director or producer on what it will take to pull off a stunt that spectacular.

It's one thing to be well rounded as a stunt person as far as skills are concerned. But to play to win today means being well rounded in the business as a whole. So take the time to study and train so you can rig your own gags whether in a car or on a wire. That way, if you don't get called for the stunt itself, perhaps you'll be called to do the rigging. It can't hurt to learn how to shoot and edit your own short film. At minimum, it will allow you to create your demo reel. You should also consider writing and directing. Longtime friend and fellow stunt professional Tim Gallin, whom I've had the pleasure to consistently work with more than 14 years now asks, "Now that you've done "*Oprah*," Angela, what's next?"

"Well," I explained, "I'm still happy in the business mainly because I'm constantly creating and accepting new challenges. Then there's that part of me who sees herself much like Arnold Schwarzenegger probably saw himself when he was a bodybuilder and a governor. I see myself as The Roc probably saw himself as a pro wrestler, and as Michael Clarke Duncan probably saw himself as someone's bodyguard. They all saw themselves as actors while doing something else.

I am Angela Meryl, one of several of stunt's leading ladies. I envision the following headline: "Leading lady of stunts turns action hero." That's what I see. That's what I feel. If Milla Jovovich can go from a supermodel gracing the covers of more than 100 magazines, surely I can go from super-stuntwoman to super-action star on television and in films.

Maybe, I'll even return as the character "Nikki" in "*Kill Bill*," and avenge the death of her mother, played by Vivica A. Fox.

But it is very clear to me that the business of film and TV is moving at a different pace and in a new direction from when my career first began. If you want to bring home the gold with some consistency, you have to look at the big picture and find a role to play in every area of the business. Although I hope you will take my advice and have at least one area of specialty, I still find it necessary to encourage you to give 100%+ towards the goal of being better than the best in everything you do so that your track record speaks for itself. Remember, your reputation will always count! Everything in life is possible when you dare to dream big and work with all your heart to make the dream your reality.

The End

Part Four

THE RESOURCE GUIDE

(Photo Credit:
Shawn Barber)

My advice is that do your homework when it comes to choosing stunt-training facilities. Investigate the person or people operating the facility. The owner and instructor(s) should have a background in performing stunts in film or on television and will most likely list them on their website to impress you. You can then visit IMDB. com (Internet Movie Data Base) to confirm their film and television credits.

While it is possible to get the basic skills from instructors that work outside the stunt industry, an experienced stunt person will have the hands on knowledge necessary for you to be aware of camera angles, reactions and other vital training to make your performance believable. So train with an experienced stunt professional.

To help get you started, I've assembled a list below, including some other examples...

Stunt Training Facilities

Film Fighting LA
310.477.8438
http://www.filmfightingla.com
Contact Robert Goodwin

FX Stunt
U.S.A. 678.492.4585
Canada 306.222.1941
http://www.fxstuntschool.com/index.html
Contact Jason (USA), Daniel (Canada)

Havoc Stunts / The Academy of Dramatic Combat
Toronto, Canada
Phone: 416-899-7966
www.havocstunts.com
www.academyofdramaticcombat.com
Contact Steve Wilsher

Impact Stunts
1150 South La Brea Ave
Los Angeles, CA. 90019
323.932.8869
www.impactstunts.com
Contact Eric Chen

Kahana Stunt School
311 Smith Road
Groveland, FL 34736
352.429.4561
http://www.kahanastunts.com/school.htm
http://kahanastuntschool.com/
Contact Mr. Kim Kahana

L.A. Stunts Training Center
Baton Rouge, LA
310.425.2848, 323.697.9174, 225.664.3198
http://www.lastuntstrainingcenter.com/
Contact Michael R. Long or Shelby Swatek

Los Angeles Fight Academy
4335 Van Nuys Blvd. #140

Sherman Oaks, CA 91403
818.446.0246
http://www.4lafa.org/

Nola Extreme Fitness
5304 Canal Blvd., New Orleans, LA. 70124
504.301.9066
http://nolaxf.com/
Contact Gino Ascani

Professional Stunt Training Center
1425 Marine Drive, Suite 207
West Vancouver, BC V7T1B9, Canada
http://www.stunt-training.com/
Contact Gary Baxley

Tempest Freerunning Academy
19821 Nordhoff Pl. #115
Los Angeles, CA 91311
818.717.0525
http://tempestacademy.com/

Rapier Wit
575 Wellington Street West
Toronto, Ontario, M5V 1G3, Canada
416.534.1947
http://www.rapierwit.com
Contact Daniel Levinson

Ring of Steel
Student Theatre Arts Complex (STAC)
University of Michigan
734.320.1147, 585.307.0402
www.ringofsteel.org
Contact Maestro Barbeau or Diane

Riot Act
Toronto, Ontario, Canada
416.817.1359
www.riotact.ca
Contact Simon Fon

Rob Radkokk EK
850.322.4577
www.radkoffek.com
Contact Rob Radkokk

UNITED STUNTMENS ASSOCIATION
206.349.8339
http://www.stuntschool.com/
Contact David Boushey

Driving Schools

Bobby Ore Motorsports
10681 US Hwy #98
Sebring, FL
863-385-1924
www.bobbyoremotorsports.com
Contact Bobby Ore

Drivers East High Performance Stunt Driving School
Wall Township, NJ
800-803-3992
www.driverseast.com
Contact Roy Farfel

Rick Seaman's Driving School
Willow Springs Raceway
Rosamond, CA
818-341-9526

www.rickseamanstuntdrivingschool.com
Contact Rick Seaman

Wagon Train Productions
560 Aviation Drive
Camarillo, CA 93010
805-890-0021, 818-774-3889
http://wagontrainproductions.com/
Contact Jim Wilkey

Martial Arts

Gokor / Hayastan MMA Academy
877-700-4656
www.gokor.com
Gokor Chivichyan & Gene LeBell

KFM CIMA Studios
16804 Oakmont Ave.
Gaithersburg,MD. 20877
240.403.0171
http://www.cima-studios.com and https://www.keysikfm.com/en
Contact Javier Carvajal, Craig Dickerson, Fernando Carvajal

Screenfighter Productions
12400 Ventura Blvd. Suite 640
Studio City Ca 91604
818.905.2111
www.screenfighter.com
Contact: Marcus Salgado

Nicky's Pro Karate/The Training Zone.
22283 Mulholland Hwy
Calabasas, CA 91302

818.225.9392
http://www.npkarate.com/

White Lotus Kung Fu Studio.
18369 Eddy Street Unit B.
Northridge CA 91325
818.993.9664
http://www.whitelotuskungfu.com/
Contact Travis Wong

98
The How To Handbook
99
The Resource Guide

Fencing

Swords Fencing Studio/Academy of Theatrical Combat
2115 N. Glen Oaks Blvd.
Burbank, CA 91504
818.840.8690
www.swordsfencingstudio.com
Contact Jan and Dan

High Falls

Bob Yerkes Productions
By invitation
Contact Teddy's Service at 323-462-2301

In addition to having credited the Russian Swing, Bob, along with colleague Dar Robinson, is responsible for creating the airbag. For 17-years Bob was also the trainer for "Circus for the Stars." He has trained just about everyone in the stunt business at one time or another. His background is the training ground for everyone from amateur to veteran professional stunt men and women who come to master high and low falls, sword fighting, trampoline, air rams and more.

Stunt Directories

If you're planning on working in the stunt industry, having a profile in a stunt directory will give you a huge advantage. In addition to being a resource for stunt coordinators attempting to locate and determine who fits the criteria of a specific search, it is a point of reference for film, commercial, print, features & television production personnel leading to the who's who of the stunt business.

Stunt directories allow you to list your performance abilities, body measurements, a short list of actors you've doubled, your stunt group along with any other group or groups to which you belong. You can chat with other members, post pictures, videos and more. Most importantly, it lists your contact information.

Consider joining multiple directories. Research them all to determine which are the most useful and helpful in meeting your career objectives. Several of the directories listed below even offer weekly and daily career tips from stunt industry veterans.

Today's stunt directories are available in print, online and often include smart phone applications.

Stunt Players Directory
www.stuntplayers.com.

Stuntphone
http://www.stuntphone.com

iStunt.com
http://istunt.com

CMG Talent
www.cmg.com

Stunt Groups for Men

Brand X
www.brandxstunts.org

Stunts Unlimited
www.stuntsunlimited.com

Stuntmen's Association of Motion Pictures
www.stuntmen.com

International Stunt Men's Association
www.isa.com

Stunt Groups for Women

V10 Stuntwomen Professionals
www.v10stunts.com

Stuntwomen's Association of Motion Pictures
www.stuntwomen.com

United Stuntwomen's Association
www.usastunts.com

Casting Services

Actors Access, Breakdown Services, Showfax
www.actorsaccess.com

Backstage The Actor's Resource (see "Casting & Jobs")
www.backstage.com

Casting Frontier
www.castingfrontier.com

Casting Networks at LA Casting
www.lacasting.com

Tips for Creating
Great Resumes and Cover Letters

- As an example, feel free to sample my resume at www.angelameryl.com and then personalize you own.
- Consider performing an internet search for "stunt resumes" to sample others.
- Creating a cover letter when targeting a stunt coordinator is a 50/50 ordeal. If you've never met the coordinator, yes, I suggest that you create a results driven cover letter. Limit it to no more than a few short paragraphs. Take a heart felt interest in your approach by researching the stunt coordinator to become somewhat familiar with his or her work. Use the same thought process if your letter is being sent to a casting director or agent and in both cases include a small enough amount of information that suggests you've done your due diligence. Definitely list your strengths and areas of specialty.

Sample Letters...

Hi Mark,
First congratulations on SWAT!

Just wanted to update you on what I've been doing since working with you on "The Wire".

- I was the stunt double for Sonja Sohn, where I drove an SUV over a curb
- I just booked national commercials JEEP and 7UP
- Currently I am working on "Kill Bill," as a stunt double for Vivica A. Fox.
- I also doubled Gabrielle Union in "Cradle to the Grave."

Please feel free to contact me through any of the above numbers. I look forward to working with you again.

Angela

****

Dear Mr. Adams,
My name is Angela Meryl and I am seeking a theatrical agent.

Commercially, I'm signed with KSA.

I just finished shooting a movie called "Havoc," where I play Dinah. I also have national commercials currently running for Toyota, Nationwide Insurance, United Airlines and Pepsi.

I look forward to meeting you and you meeting me. 🤳

Contact numbers are listed above for convenience.

Thanks for your consideration.

Angela Meryl

Stunt Gear Resources

Amspec for harnesses, rachets, back packs
5917 Noble Avenue,
Van Nuys, CA 91411
818-782-6165
http://www.amspecinc.com/

Climbing Sutra for specialty harnesses
http://www.climbingsutra.com/

Stunt Equipment Shop
(805) 501-4028
http://www.stuntequipmentshop.com/index.php

Photos, Clips and Demo Reel Tips and Resources

- Word of Mouth: The best possible resource for locating a good photographer or editor to help you create your demo reel is by word of mouth. Check around with friends in the business or via social media to share resources.
- Backstage The Actors Resource: The classified section of Backstage The Actors Resource includes advertisements for photographers. www.backstage. com
- Casting Agents: When considering photographers, know that casting agents often allow photographers to advertise in their offices
- LA Casting: Membership based casting services available through LA Casting offer resources including photographers, coaches for acting and

music, industry related seminars and workshops and more at $14.95 monthly, plus a $20 set up fee. At $79.95 pre-paid, you'll get six months of service with no setup fee. www.lacasting.com

- Actors Access: At Actors Access, registration is free. The list of referrals includes airchecks. An aircheck is a media monitoring service that provides customers with a recording of an entire television program. From the program you can extract a clip of your performance. Actors Access will also post the clip on your account where casting directors and agents can view. For those who have no clips, Actors Access also provides a service called "Scene Slate," where they will shoot and edit a scene for you. Hosting Slate is another service where you can choose from a show template and create a video with you as the host. On the website, go to the "Learn More" and see "Actors Slate." www.actorsaccess.com

- Edit Plus: Edit Plus will help you assemble your clips into a demo reel. www.editplus.tv

- Hulu: If unsure whether or not your appearance in a movie or TV show made it past the final edit, you can locate and watch the production on www.hulu.com prior to any further plans to get a copy of the clip for your reel.

PART FIVE

GLOSSARY OF STUNT INDUSTRY TERMINOLOGY

(Photo Credit: Shawn Barber)

Above the Line. A budgetary term for movies and TV. The line refers to money budgeted for creative talent, such as actors, writers, directors, and producers.

Acting Resume. Focuses exclusively on acting and establishes your credibility as an actor by listing your acting experience and training as well as promote you as an actor to agents and casting directors.

Action. A director's cue to begin filming.

A.D. An assistant director, and usually part of a hierarchy, whose duties will include helping to set up shots, coordinating and writing call sheets, and directing and corralling extras.

ADR. Automatic digital recording, or additional dialogue recording.

Airbrushing. A photographic process whereby certain flaws in a picture are gently blown off of a master print.

Air Checks. A recording made of a televised show on 3/4" tape to be used for demo reels.

Apple Boxes. Wooden crates that elevate either an actor, a cameo or furniture on a set.

Atmosphere. Another term for "extras" or "background artists".

Audition. A formally arranged session (usually by appointment through an agent) for an actor to display his or her talents when seeking a role in an upcoming production of a play, film or television project, usually to a casting director, director or producers.

Avail. A courtesy extended by a performer or agent to a producer indicating availability to work a certain job. Avails have no legal or contractual status.

Background. Another term for extras or atmosphere. Back-to-One. Direction given by the Assistant Director after a take. It means to go back to the position which you were in at the beginning of the scene.

Beat (theater). Pause. Also used in fighting and Acting Best Boy. They are either part of the grip or electrical department. They are the right hand persons of the Key Grip or Gaffer.

Billing. The size of an actor's role such as starring or guest starring. Also, where the actor's name will be placed in the credits and if the name will be shown on the screen alone or with others.

Bit Part. A small part, usually consisting of a few lines. Blocking. In rehearsals, actors practice the required movements, in a pattern or along a path, for a given scene that allows them to avoid any awkward positions, such as one actor walking in front of another actor or standing with his or her back to the camera.

Blocking Stage. Rehearsing as if you were on a stage but these early rehearsals are typically held in warehouses, parking lots or someone's living space, naturally without actual props or sets.

Blue Screen. Also sometimes called Green Screen, it is a blank screen which acts as the backdrop to live action. Any background can be laid into the background and give the impression that the live action was really happening in the context of the blue screen.

Body-Shot Picture. Subject is seen in an outfit (body suit, work-out clothes, dance attire, bathing suit) or performing a special skill/stunt (martial arts, surf boarding, skiing, dancing) that accentuates their body in some way.

Booking. A confirmed session indicating you have a job.

Book Out. A call to all of your agents to let them know you are working, traveling or are unavailable for auditions or a job.

Borderless. A photograph that takes up the full space of the paper with no white edges.

Boom. The Overhead microphone used to record actors' voices.

Boom Mike. A microphone on the end of a pole, held above actor's heads to record dialogue.

Boot Legging. The unauthorized recording and selling of a performance of a movie or song.

Breaking Character. Stepping out of the scene which you are doing.

Breakdown Services. A fee-based service provided to agents that offers a daily breakdown of roles for each production submitted by participating casting directors.

Breaking-up. Out-of-place laughter by an actor on stage.

Broad. An exaggerated performance.

Bump Up. An upgrade in pay and billing when an Extra says a few words or other special activity in a scene.

Buyout. A one-time payment for shooting and airing a commercial.

Callback. A second audition where an actor is either presented to the producer and director or, in the case of commercials, is filmed on tape again for final consideration.

Call Sheet. The daily sheet for a production that lists all the scenes to be shot that day as well as actor and crew arrival times.

Call Time. The time you are supposed to report to the set.

Calling Service. As pertains to extras, a company that helps to book them on extra jobs.

Camera Right. When looking into the camera, your left.

Camera Left. When looking into the camera, your right.

Cans. Slang term meaning headphones.

Cast. As a noun, generally refers to the group of actors performing in a particular production. As a verb, refers to the final status of an actor that has won a role or part in a production over other competing performers.

Casting. When a casting director puts out the news that he needs to fill a certain role that requires an approximate age range and appearance such as a certain ethnicity, height, build or look.

Character Role. A supporting role with pronounced or eccentric characteristics.

Circle Takes. A director's favorite or most usable filming of a particular scene. Used to expedite the editing process.

Class A Network Spot. Commercial airing at prime time on a major network. Residuals are highest for this type of spot.

Cold Reading. Delivering a speech or acting a scene at an audition without having read it beforehand.

Colored Pages. Pages onto which script rewrites are copied.

Commercial Head or 3/4 Shot. Used to seek a commercial agent, and on commercial auditions. The shot usually depicts the subject as perky and upbeat with bright energetic eyes.

Commission. Percentage of income paid by actors to their representative. If it is an agent, the amount cannot be over 10% for a union contract; if it is a manager, the percentage is unregulated, but is traditionally 15-20%.

Comml. Abbreviation for "commercial."

Composite. A type of head shot popular in the commercial industry which positions several different images of the subject together on one 8" x 10" spread giving casting directors a quick way to determine how the subject will look

Composite card. Also known as a "comp card," it is a grouping of 3-5 photos of a model on one sheet which includes the model's statistics and sometimes biographical information. Used for promotional purposes, the photos should include at least one head shot and show poses which highlight the model's best features.

Concept Meeting. A gathering of the producer, director and casting director to reach an agreement about the look and quality of each character in a script.

Conflicts. Being under contract for two conflicting products. This is prohibited for union commercials. An advertiser would never want one person on the air advertising both the company's product and a competitor's.

Console. The audio board or control panel that allows the engineer to direct the audio signal to the recorders, and to combine the various audio components into the final mix.. Continuity. Matching action in each take of a scene with the same props, dialogue, extras, wardrobe, make up, etc. Control Booth. A glass-enclosed area full of equipment where an engineer and director sit during looping and dubbing sessions.

Coogan Laws. Guidelines created by SAG and named after child-actor, Jackie Coogan, for the work and pay schedules of children.

Copy. A slang term for "dialogue" or "script."

Copy Points. The items in a script that require particular attention, and therefore particular interpretation by the voice actor.

Cover Set. Set which is always ready for shooting on a moment's notice. If a film crew is scheduled to shoot outside, and it rains, they move to the cover set. Co-Writing. Joint authorship of one work by two or more writers.

Craft Service. The food table on a set, or refers to the person(s) who handle the food. Crew. Everyone on the set who is contributing to the production, in addition to the cast.

CU. A close-up shot.

Cue (theatrical). A line of dialogue, actions or sound, onstage or off, that tells an actor it is time to enter, exit, move across stage, begin speaking, etc.

Cue Cards. The large flash cards that have an actor's script printed on them and that are read when auditioning for a role in a TV commercial.

Cut. (Film) The director's cue to stop filming.

Cuts. Lines, speeches, songs, or any other element in a printed script left out of a particular production.

DAT. Digital Audio Tape.

Day-out-of-Days. Schedule made by the Assistant Director (AD) assigning time slots for when certain people or things will work on set.

Day-Player. Someone who is hired at SAG scale (minimum) for the day.

Day Shot. A specific scene in the script to be filmed or taped while the sun is out.

Delivery/Distribution Manager (film). Once you have a distribution deal in place, "Delivery", a technical term, is next. It consists of supplying the physical elements such as the interpositive, internegative, soundtracks, video masters, stills and slides and the legal elements such as copyright registration, rights documents insurance, copyright and title searches and talent agreements.

Demo. Short for "demonstration," a demo can be a sample tape of a talent's voice used to show his or her abilities.

Demo Firm. An organization specializing in the production of demo tapes.

Demo Tape. An audiocassette, audio CD or DVD recording of an actor's voice demonstrating voice acting abilities.

Dialogue-less Commercials. Used to emphasize a visual image with the spoken words of an announcer as the only recorded sound.

Diaphragm. The lower part of the lungs, filling the abdominal space, that supports the voice when actors and singers breathe correctly on stage.

Diction. Clear, sharp pronunciation of words, especially of consonants.

Director. Charged with staging a play or musical, who coordinates all onstage aspects of the production, including the performances of the actor. In television and film production, this person influences the actions of actors and action sequences during filming, and supervises editing afterward.

Director's Cut. Film that is slightly or drastically different from the final cut that the studio ultimately releases.

Distributor/Distribution Arranger (film). Independent producers are not usually involved in the distribution of films. Distribution is still the domain of the Hollywood-based major studios that generate more than 90% of U.S. box office, but there are also smaller distributors and independent sales agents who handle independent productions. There are also non-profit organizations that can lend a hand in various ways.

Donut. A type of spot that has prerecorded material at the beginning and at the end with a "hole" in the middle for the voice part. The parts can be reversed as well, with the voice being the donut and the pre-recorded material in the hole.

Double-take. An exaggerated facial response to another actor's words or actions, usually used for comic effect.

Downstage. The area of the stage closest to the audience.

D.P. Director of photography, in charge of designing and lighting the shot.

Drive To. Monies paid to an actor by a production company for driving to location other than a studio lot.

Drop/Pick-up. Term used when an actor is dropped from, then picked-up by payroll; this can only be done when there are ten working days between the drop and pick-up work dates and can only be done one time per actor per project.

Dub. An audio or video copy. Also called a "dupe" (short for duplicate).

Earprompter. A small tape recorder system which the entire script is recorded and is transmitted to an earpiece through a loop around the neck. It is activated by a foot or hand control. Known in the industry as "the ear."

ECU. Extreme close-up.

Employee For Hire. Contractual basis whereby a motion picture producer or company employs a composer or lyricist to create music or songs for a movie with copyright ownership to be retained by the producer or company.

Engineer. Individual who operates studio equipment during the recording of a song.

Exclusive Songwriting Contract. A contract which prohibits the songwriter from writing for more than one publisher.

EXT. Seen at the beginning of a new scene description in a script, refers to Exterior.

Exterior Shot. A scene filmed or taped out of doors..

False Start. Term used to describe a take in which the talent makes an error within the first couple of lines. The take is usually stopped, and a new take is slated.

Favored Nations. An agreement which means that all terms are equal among all actors.

Featured Role. A co-starring role where you may have played a large role but weren't necessarily the main character.

Finding Your Light. An actor's ability to sense when he or she is properly placed in respect to stage lighting.

Fire in the Hole. An explosion or gunshot is ready to occur.

First Refusal. A request to hold an actor for a given day. It is not binding for either the producer or you. It is more of a sign of interest than an availability request, and it is not as good as a booking.

First Team. The actual cast members who are being used in a given scene.

Flap. In animation, movement of the mouth. If the talking stops and the character's mouth keeps moving, an actor will be called in to add either internally, at the beginning, or at the end of the line so that the mouth flaps match the rhythm of the speech.

Flashing. What is said when taking a flash picture.

Forced Call. Making an actor or crew member come to work without the required turn-around time.

Generation. The process whereby each time you copy a piece of film or tape it losses some clarity.

Golden Time. Refers to overtime paid after working sixteen hours straight, equal to one's daily rate every hour.

Green Lit. The process that follows after a script has been developed and moves into production. Production involves building sets, designing costumes, measuring and fitting actors for costumes, and rehearsals.

Green Lighted. When a studio commits to starting a project.

Grip. Someone who handles, carries, moves, and stores lighting, electrical, and other equipment on the set. Guards. These are the positions taken by the fighters at the beginning of the fight, from which they subsequently either attack or defend. Guards will be described according to which of the fighter's arms and feet are forward and which behind, together with the position, angulation and direction of their weapon.

Ham. An actor who gives a very broad or exaggerated performance.

Head Shot. An 8" x 10" photograph that acts as your calling card for securing television, film and theatrical work, showing your face as it actually appears. The head shot should capture your best and most unique physical features, while still remaining true to your actual image.

Hiatus. Time of year when the cast and crew of a television series is on vacation.

High-Speed Dub. A tape copy that is made at several times normal speed. Often used in reference to tape duplication.

High speed dubs are often less costly and have a quicker turn-around time than real time or at speed dubs. They can be susceptible to problems, so always check your dubs before releasing them to prospective clients.

Hitting Your Marks. The ability to physically stop on a preset mark or put down the product in an exact spot.

Hold. When an actor is being paid, but is not working.

Hold Over. When a director decides to use an actor for an extra day not originally scheduled.

Holding Area. A place where extras are kept on a set or location.

Honey Wagon. A bank of dressing and mini-bathroom rooms attached together and pulled by a tractor trailer to a shooting location.

Hot Mike. A microphone that is turned on.

Ink. To sign a contract.

Insert. A form of pick-up where a short segment of the script is reread from one point to another.

INT. Seen at the beginning of a new scene description in a script, refers to Interior.

Interior Shot. A scenic shot inside a sound stage or inside a set on location.

Internship/Apprenticeship. Situations in which aspiring artists receive training and perform designated tasks in creative, administrative and technical areas. They are offered by most nonprofit theaters and by mostly all summer stock theaters.

In The Can. A phrase borrowed from the film business and used in voice-overs. When a good take is achieved, it is considered ready for processing or "in the can." It generally means that the director has the take he wants.

In-The-Round. A theater in which the audience is seated on all four sides of a central stage.

Laugh Track. The laughter of a live audience of a situation comedy or other television show that actors are performing in front of, that is recorded to be played back when the show is aired.

Laundry List. A long series of copy points in a script. The object for the talent is to read the points with varying emphasis so they don't sound like a list.

Lead Role. Considered a starring role in a production.

License. As a noun, it means a legal permit; as a verb, it is to authorize by legal permit.

Line Producer. Concerned with the day-to-day details of finishing a project or just keeping the project moving forward smoothly and on schedule.

Lithography. A printing process as opposed to a photographic process used to inexpensively reproduce a large quantity of headshots.

Local. A commercial airing in only one city, generally close to where it is cast. Or a person being hired in their home state where they are registered with S.A.G

Long-form TV. Movies of the Week (MOW) or miniseries.

Looping. The art of matching lip movements and vitality of action in a scene. Dialogue that is added in post-production on a sound stage. Groups of people who work together to provide additional dialogue for a scene.

Magic Hour. The time of day when the sun casts a light which DPs have referred to as magic; a choice, for a brief period of time, during which filmmakers have to shoot.

Manager. One who guides an artist in the development of his/her career. Same as artist or personal manager.

Mannerisms. Gestures, facial expressions, and vocal tricks that a particular actor uses again and again in different roles.

Mark. Exact locations of an actor's feet on the floor during sequences of a shot.

Master. The original recording. The tape from which dubs are made. Also, a finished recording of the song from which records are pressed and distributed to radio stations and record stores.

Meal Penalty. Additional monies paid if a working cast or crew member has not been fed after the six hours allotted by union contracts.

Method Acting. An internalized form of acting that uses experiences from an actor's personal life to help produce onstage emotion.

Mike. Attaching a wireless transmitter to an actor's body or clothes to record dialogue.

Miming. Acting out.

Mix. The final audio product combining all the elements into one composite soundtrack. "Mix" also applies to the act of creating the mix. This is sometimes referred to as the "mixdown."

Monologue. A speech used by an actor to demonstrate his or her ability at an audition.

MOS. Without sound, attributed to a German director who pronounced it, "Mit out sound."

Mouth Noise. Also known as "clicks and pops." A dry mouth produces much more mouth noise than a damp one. Cigarette smoking also contributes to a dry mouth.

The less mouth noise you have, the less editing has to be done later.

Moviola. A projection machine that reduces film to a small viewing screen.

Must Join. A situation in which an actor has used up the 30-day grace period to join a union and upon hiring for the next job must join that union as mandated by the Taft-Hartley law.

National. A commercial airing everywhere in the United States.

Neutral Demo. A demo that doesn't sound like it's for one particular artist, but best represents the song whereby it can be recorded by anybody.

Night Shot. A scene specified in the script to be filmed when it is dark out.

Non-Linear Editing. Putting scenes together on a computer using film editing software capable of moving them around, and/or out of order, for ease in building a demo tape, or a scene in a movie or commercial.

Notes. Instructions, usually regarding changes in an actor's blocking or performance, given after a rehearsal by the director, musical director, choreographer or stage manager.

Off-book. When an actor knows his or her lines and no longer needs to carry the script.

Off-Camera. A part for which you supply your voice to a TV spot or video presentation.

Off-Card. A union actor working on a non-union project is known to be working 'off-card.'

On-Camera. A part in a TV spot or video production where you actually appear on screen. It pays more than offcamera voice-over, but often requires more work, as well as applying make-up.

On Hold. A situation that occurs when an actor is contracted to be available for the next day's shoot but will not have to report to the set until called.

On Location. Place other than a studio lot where filming is done.

On-or-About. A date which implies three different days, giving production twenty-four hours before and after the on-or-about date to start an actor.

'Open Audition. Audition open to the public.

Open Casting Calls. Auditions open to anyone.

Option. Acquiring the rights to a story, such as a current events, true-life story, that guarantees that no one else can work with the party who sold the story. Options typically last for a year or less.

Out Takes. Parts of an original filming or taping that will not be used in editing the finished product.

P.A. A production assistant who usually gophers and manages the extras.

Pace. The speed at which a scene is played.

Packager. One who selects and combines talent for shows.

Pan. A very bad review from a critic.

Pantomime. Being silent, yet appearing to talk.

Parent Union. The first professional union you join; subsequent unions are sister unions.

Pausing For Effect. A deliberate pause within or between lines, used by an actor to call special attention to a moment.

Pay-per-airing. Monies paid to an actor each time a television commercial is shown.

Per Diem. Money given to actors and crew when on location to cover the expense of food and other personal incidentals.

Period. Project not set in current time period.

Period Piece. A play from an earlier time, played in the style, costumes, and sets representing the period it depicts.

Phone Patch. A session where the talent and the director are in separate locations. The session must be "patched" over telephone lines so everyone can hear everyone else. Photo Double. An actor, usually an extra, used in place of a principal actor who is either unavailable or only seen partially, and never has any speaking lines.

Physical Film Producer. Once you have a script, director, cast and financing, you can then proceed to make a movie. Details and procedural steps will include: setting up a production company (if one isn't already in place); hiring employees or engaging independent contractors; setting up accounting and payroll services, becoming signatory with the talent and craft guilds, finding location; clearing the script and title of any obstacles; while shooting, getting the best performances from cast, crew and director; while watching budgets and time; in post-production, helping to edit shot footage into the story line.

Pick-Up. To start reading the script from a place other than the beginning. A "pick-up" is usually when the top part of the script has been successfully completed and only the end needs to be worked on. Narration scripts are usually done in a series of pick-ups. Pick-up can also be a request to read faster. Pick-up Shot. Small parts of a scene that are re-shot, usually because all angles were not captured satisfactorily during the first shooting.

Picture Car. A car being filmed.

Pilot Presentation. A one-day shoot to give a network an idea of the look and feel of a proposed program available to be produced into a new series.

Pipeline. A listing or schedule of movie projects in some stage of production.

Pirating. The unauthorized reproduction and selling of sound recordings (i.e., records, tapes, CDs).

Pitching. The action a producer takes in trying to convince a studio to invest money in a project based on a concept or a script.

Playbill. A theatrical program in which an actors' biography appears.

Playwright. The writer of the work up for production, who in theater, may wield as much power as the director, getting involved in casting and rehearsals.

Plot. Storyline.

Plus Ten. The 10% commission negotiated by an agent, specifically referring to the 10% added to the base pay negotiated for the actor. (If the job pays only scale, the agent can not take a percentage unless he has negotiated the contract to be on a plus-ten basis).

Post. A short form of "post production." This is the term applied to all the work that goes into a production after the talent leaves. This includes such processes as editing, multi-tracking, music selection, adding special effects and mixing.

P.O.V. The point of view that is filmed, usually referring to that of one of the actors.

Pre-reads. An advance reading by a casting director who is unfamiliar with an actor's work prior to taking the actor to meet a producer or director.

Presence. An actor's ability to command attention onstage, even when surrounded by other actors.

Press. The manufacture of a large quantity of records duplicated from a master for commercial sale.

Press Kit. A presentation including newspaper clippings, review of movie, television, musical and theater productions, a biography, headshot and resume given to the media and interested industry professionals. Also called a press package.

Principal Player. An actor with lines, paid at least SAG scale.

Print. Director's cue that the shot was good enough to "print" or use.

Producer. The individual who oversees the making of a single or long playing record, radio, television or stage show from inception to completion.

Production. The technical aspects of the Film and T.V industry, including sound systems and lighting requirements as well as video and recording process.

Project Developer. The function in this role is to write or supervise the writing of a screenplay that can attract a director, cast and financing. If the screenplay is to be based on material owned by someone else, or is co-authored with others, the rights for it must be optioned or acquired.

Projection. An actor's ability to use his or her voice so that it can be clearly heard in the back rows of a theater; also used in reference to the emotions an actor wishes to convey.

Project Financier. Upon securing a director and principal actor, production financing is next. Sources of independent financing are family and friends, equity investors, distributors in the form of domestic studios and foreign sales agents, banks, foreign subsidies and tax incentives. A lawyer is absolutely needed during this phase.

Project Packager. When a screenplay is finalized the film must be packaged and financing secured. The film package consists of the script, director, producer, and cast, as well as the budget and production schedule. The budget and schedule are flexible and usually can be changed and adapted as time goes by. However, it is a good idea to have a budget range in mind during the development process. But overall, the fundamental issues of this process are when and how to get talent.

Promoter. One who secures talent from an agent for the production and presentation of a performance; the primary risk taker in the event.

Proof Sheet. After a roll of film is shot and developed, it is printed onto sheets of 8 1/2 x 11 or 11 x 14 inch paper, holding up to 36 exposures. Use a photographer's loop to check the lighting and focus.

Props. Any moveable object, from a letter to a sword, used by an actor during a performance.

Protection. You may be asked to "do another take for protection." This means that you have given the director a take she likes but she wants you to do it again to make sure it was the best. Also referred to as "insurance."

Publication. The printing and distribution of copies of a work to a public by sole or other transfer of ownership, or by rental, lease or lending.

Public Domain. Unprotected by copyright due to an expired copyright or caused by an invalid copyright notice.

Publicist. A person hired to create awareness of a person or project.

Queued Up. Previewing a tape and having it set to start playing at the beginning of a scene.

Raked Stage. A tilted performing area, usually specially constructed, with its upstage space raised higher than the downstage space.

Reader. Another actor who is paid, or volunteers, to help the casting office by playing all the other characters during an audition so the casting director can concentrate on the actor being screened.

Read-through. When the director and the actors sit around a table and read through the entire script to get familiar with the story, their roles, and their fellow actors.

Recall. When at the end of a work day, a production company decides to use your services for an additional day.

Recurring Role. Typically found on television shows where your character pops up from time to time in a few episodes of a regular show.

Reel Or Tape. A video tape compilation of an actor's best work.

Regional. A commercial airing in a part of the United States.

Release (marketing). The issuing of a record by the record company, or a film by a studio.

Release (legal). Legal document releasing producer from liability, usually refers to talent allowing the producer to use his or her likeness on film and soundtrack.

Residuals. Also known as royalties, these are additional monies to actors (but not extras) for film, TV or commercial work airing on local television or international television stations.

Retouching. A photographic process whereby certain flaws in a picture are covered up or removed.

Rider (to Contract). An addition to a performer's union contract that outlives a special circumstance for pay, and airing privileges given to the production company by a union.

Right-to-Work. Ability to accept employment without joining a labor union, usually referring to states whose labor codes insure that right.

Right-to-Work state. In a right-to-work state, actors who have not joined a union may do both union and nonunion work. Companies cannot refuse to hire an actor because they do not belong to a union or do not want to join a union. This does not mean that a union actor in one of these states my do both union and nonunion work; union actors must still abide by union rules. The right-to-work states are: Alabama, Arizona, Arkansas, Florida, Georgia, Indiana, Iowa, Kansas, Louisiana, Mississippi, Nebraska, Nevada, North Carolina, North Dakota, South Carolina, Tennessee, Texas, Utah, Virginia and Wyoming.

Rolling. Cameras have been turned on and film is rolling.

Roomtone. The sound a room makes without anyone in it. Everyone has a different sound, so recording in the same room is sometimes critical when trying to match voice parts from one session to another.

Run Throughs. Rehearsals before the actual filming of a scene.

Rush Calls. A last minute call by an agency to an actor for an audition or a job.

SAG-eligible. A non-union actor who is eligible to join SAG by being cast in a principal role, being a member of an affiliated union and having had a principal role under that union's jurisdiction, or performing three days of union extra work. Also known as a "must join."

SAG-franchised. Status of an agent or agency that has signed papers with SAG and agrees to operate within SAG guidelines.

SASE. Means "self-addressed, stamped envelope."

Scale. Minimum SAG daily wage for principal actors.

Scene Study and Analysis. A pre-audition practice of studying a few pages of a script ahead of time.

Score. The compilation of pages of sheet music that contains all the music for a show.

Scoring. Music added to help fill scenes or dialogue cut by a director during post-production.

Screen Test. A type of audition during which an actor will be filmed performing a particular role, often not on the set or in proper wardrobe or makeup.

Second Meal. The meal served six hours after the end of lunch.

Second Take. Being taped or filmed an additional time in a scene or audition allowing an actor to change his or her performance.

Second Team. A group of stand-ins who take the primary actors' places allowing them to rest during lighting changes and camera rehearsals.

Session Fee. The money you are paid for the initial day's work on a commercial. It is usually a sale amount.

Set. As a noun, the physical design of the stage area within which the actors perform; as a verb, to make permanent the way in which a scene is being played.

Set Call Time. The moment the actor is expected to be in front of the camera in full make up and wardrobe, ready to begin working.

Set Dressing. Items placed in the scene to complement the story.

SFX. Abbreviation for sound effects. Sometimes also written as EFX. or FX.

Shoot Around You. Shooting other scenes in a script until a particular actor is available.

Showcase (theatrical). An evening of scenes either prepared and rehearsed ahead of time or done as a cold reading for industry professionals who may cast the actors in roles.

Sides. Designated scenes pulled out of an entire script to be used for auditions.

Signator(y). A company which has signed an agreement with a union, agreeing to adhere to all the rules of that union, whether it be SAG, AFTRA, DGA, etc.

Sign-in Sheet. Exhibit E SAG/AFTRA Audition Report which an actor fills out and initials upon arrival at a casting office.

Signing Out. The act of entering the time you exit an audition on the Exhibit E Sign-in Sheet.

Silent Bit. When an actor or extra performs a noticeable or required action in a scene, but with no lines.

Slate. An audible announcement of the take number recorded ahead of your read. The slate aids the engineer in finding the favorite takes for editing.

Small. A very subtle performance by an actor.

Sister Union. One or more additional unions you join after the first one. The first union you join is your parent union.

Size Card. A form filled out at commercial casting sessions to inform wardrobe people of your clothing sizes.

Slate. The act of stating your name and agency on a commercial audition while being videotaped. Slice-of-Life Commercial. A miniature play that quickly identifies a problem and just as quickly offers a solution.

Sloppy Border. A type of border surrounding a photograph that looks as though it were painted on with a paint brush and has an uneven quality.

Spec. Short for speculative. It usually means volunteering your services and postponing payment until a project sells.

Spec Script. Several writers may work together to put words to an idea, and in the process create a script in hopes that someone will buy and produce the script concept. Also, a production company may hire writers to create a script from a story idea that they already own.

Speed. Exclamation that indicates the film and the audiotape are running simultaneously at the correct speed.

Spokesperson Commercial. Uses an authority figure (usually very recognizable or with professional credentials) to lend credibility to a product right away.

Spot. A commercial for radio or television.

Squibs. Radio-controlled explosive pockets of fake blood attached to an actor's body.

Stage Left. The side of the stage that is to the actor's left as he or she faces the audience.

Stage Right. The side of the stage that is to the actor's right as he or she faces the audience.

Stand-in. After a scene has been set for the next sequence of filming – moving props, checking the sound, adjusting the lighting, and arranging different camera angels – a crew of actors other than the principal ones are used to go through the actions that the principal ones will follow, such as walking through a door, sitting in a chair, picking up a object, etc.; an actor who has a similar height, build and look of the principal actor, is used (instead of using the time of the principal) where the principal is going to stand while the crew makes sure that lighting and camera angles are okay.

Station 12. Report which a casting director must obtain from

SAG before employing one of its actors.

Storyboard. A frame-by-frame artist's drawing of key scenes with the dialogue printed underneath serving as a rough plan for the way the commercial or film should appear and what camera angles the director should use.

Strike. To remove something from a set, or tear it down.

Studio (film). Monolithic "Hollywood" entity that oversees the approval of concepts leading to the creation and production of major motion pictures.

Studio (sound). An audio isolation room where the talent performs, with an adjoining control room.

Studio Hire. Union term for actors who work in the same area in which they are hired or reside.

Studios/Studio School. Acting schools usually founded by and built around a single master teacher and his or her vision or theory of the acting craft. They generally offer a variety of classes that can be taken in eight- or ten-week segments, or longer terms.

Stunt. A dangerous scene; alternately, a publicity event designed to call attention to a project or a particular actor.

Subtext. The subtleties between the lines of a scene.

Supporting Role. Usually a small role where you had some acting and speaking parts.

Stunt Pay. Additional hazard money paid to a actor or stuntperson to perform dangerous scenes. Also known as an adjustment.

Syndication. A popular television show is sold to be broadcast in a local or regional market.

Taft-Hartley Law. A law that allows non-union actors to work under a union contract for their first role. After that, they must join the union.

Tag. A short portion of a spot, usually placed at the end. A tag may say something such as, "Available at all OfficeMax outlets through Sunday." Tags are often delivered by a voice talent different from those in the main body of the ad.

Take. The attempted shooting of a scene. The "attempted" refers to the usual circumstance in which it usually takes several takes to get the scene right from the actor, director, camera person and sound mixers standpoint.

Talent Scout. Hired by studios and casting agencies to search for fresh star talent.

Talkback. The system that allows people in the control room to talk with the talent in the studio.

Tear Sheets. An actual copy of a print ad torn out of a newspaper or magazine and put in a model's portfolio.

Telegraphing. Broad charade-type actions used by inexperienced actors to get a point across.

Teleprompter. A machine placed in front of the lens of a camera on which an actor's dialogue is projected. The dialogue scrolls by and is read when at eye level.

Test Audience. Special screenings used to gauge the reaction of the group, and help determine certain scenes to be dropped and new ones added.

Test Commercial. A commercial that will be aired in a small area and monitored for its effectiveness. You must be told that the commercial will be a test commercial before the audition.

Test Photographers. Photographers willing to barter their services at a reduced rate to help themselves and a new model build their respective portfolios.

Theatrical Head or 3/4 Shot. A shot that captures a view of you from your head to your knees. The shot generally does not portray the subject with a full smile, but rather an intense look, or showing attitude.

Track. One of the several components of special recording tape that contains recorded sounds, which is mixed with the other tracks for a finished recording of the song; the recording of all the instruments or voice of a particular music section; music and/or voices previously recorded.

Trades. Industry newspapers and magazines read by all professionals to keep up with trends and news in the entertainment business.

Trailer. A mobile dressing room for an actor sometimes in a camper. Also known as Honey Wagon.

Transparencies. The slide form of a photograph.

Treatment. A shortened version to a full script which includes a short description of the story and the characters involved, and typically ranges from one to six pages in length. Turnaround. Cast and crew rest time, from wrap until next day's call time.

Two-Shot. Camera shot with two people in frame.

Type Casting. Assigning a role to an actor on the basis of his or her surface appearance or personality.

Typed-out. The elimination of an actor during auditions because of such obvious features as height, weight or age.

Under-Five (U/5). An acting role designation calling for five lines or less on AFTRA shows. This category has a specific pay rate, which is less than a day-player.

Understudy. An actor, often playing a small role, who learns another role, so as to be able to perform it if the regular actor is ill.

Union Scale. Minimum wage scale earned in employment by members of AFTRA, AF of M, SAG, etc.

Upgrade. A pay-rate increase, usually from "extra" status to "principal" status.

UPM. Unit Production Manager.

Upstage. The rear area of the stage farthest from the audience; also used to describe an actor's attempt to distract audience attention from what another actor is doing.

Usage Fee. The practice of assigning each city in the U.S. points based on population. An actors residuals on television commercials are calculated based on the accumulation of these points in 13-week cycles.

Verse. The selection of a song that precedes the chorus or is the A section in AABA pattern songs. The Verse follows the Vamp and is the first vocalizing of the text of the song. The Verse seldom contains heavyweight musical material. Since it is so scored in order to give preeminence to the information contained in the lyric, most often Verses can be ad libded without effort.

Video Toaster. A popular computer editing system for actor's demo tapes.

Voice Over. The act of providing one's voice to a media project. Called voice-over because the voice is usually mixed over the top of music and sound effects.

Walk Through. To perform a role at less-than-usual intensity, such as during a technical rehearsal; also used critically, as in "he walked it," for a lazy performance at a matinee.

Walking Meal. Usually second meal; company doesn't actually stop filming, but food is provided.

Walla. The sound of many voices talking at once, such as at a party or in a restaurant. Also known as "walla walla," this old sound effects term is derived from the idea that if a group of people got together and just kept saying "walla" over and over, it would create a good sound ambiance for a crowded scene.

Wardrobe List. The important list of clothes to wear for different styles of pictures.

Weather Day. If the weather is not right for the shoot and it does not take place, it will be postponed until the weather day. When this happens, you will receive a half day's pay for each canceled day.

Weekly Player. Actor being paid on a weekly contract.

Wet. A voice or sound with reverb added to it.

Wild Line. A single line from the script that is reread several times in succession until the perfect read is achieved. Wild lines are often done in a series. The slate may say something such as, "This is wild line pick-up take twelve A, B & C." This means you will read the line three times on this slate without interruption by the director. It is considered "wild" because it is done separately from the entire script. In video or film work, they are lines that occur when the camera is on something other than you. They are "wild" because it is not necessary for them to be in sync with your mouth.

Wild Spot. A commercial that runs on a non-network station, or a spot that runs on a network sation but airs between scheduled programming.

Will-Notify. A call given to actors when call time is uncertain, indicates an actor will work, but no specific call time has been determined.

Windscreen. A foam cover or fabric guard placed over a microphone to help prevent popped "P's" and other plosive sounds. Sometimes called a "windsock" or "pop filter."

Workshop. A place for putting together and polishing a production. Also, a place where one can receive instruction and practice in directing, acting, and stagecraft.

Work Vouchers. A paper given to an Extra at the time of check-in. It must be filled out and turned in at the end of the day of shooting to receive wages.

Wrap. The end of the days shooting of film.

Writer's Signature. Unique style of the writer.

ACKNOWLEDGEMENTS

(Photo Credit: Shawn Barber)

H ad it not been for so many daring women in whose footsteps I walk today, there's no way I would have achieved so many career highs.

To the many women such as Bessie Coleman – the first African-American woman to earn a pilot's license, who later became a stunt pilot; Jeannie Epper, who doubled lead actresses in two hit TV series – "Wonder Woman" and "The Bionic Woman" – with stunt credits dating as far back as 1964; and Jadie David, the modern-day trailblazer whose work includes doubling for the legendary Pam Grier in such hits as "Foxy Brown," I follow in your footsteps and owe each of you a debt of gratitude.

I could also fill an entire book with names of industry professionals and friends I refer to as my colleagues – all of whom I owe a debt of gratitude for anything and everything from a word of encouragement to a word of advice that probably helped to save my life on one stunt or another. To you all, I say thank you from the bottom of my heart.

In no particular order, I've listed individuals below at the risk that I will probably have forgotten someone's name who is very dear and /or has contributed to my career in some beneficial way. If you're inadvertently omitted, let me say to you right now, thank you, thank you and thank you.

Having issued that disclaimer, I offer my appreciation to the following: Lance Gilbert, Craig Baxley, George M. Ruge, Kerry Rossall, Mike Smith, Mike Russo, Mike Massa, Andy Gill, Merritt Yohnka, Jim Wilkey, Blaize Corrigan, Gregg Brazel, Artie Malesci, Danny Weselis, Terry James, George Aguilar, Doug Coleman, Vince Deadrick Jr., Charlie Croughwell, Webster Whinery, Joel Kramer, Terry Leonard, Danny Aiello III, Mellisa Stubbs, Doug Crosby, Dennis Scott, Lou Simon, Phil Culotta, Wally Crowder, Noon Orsati, Bob Brown, Larry Lee, Johnny Martin, Scott Wilde, Master Wo Ping, Keith Adams, Lubomir Misak, Monty Simons, Chris Howell, Dan Bradley, Jimmy Romano, Jack Gill, Jim Vickers, Ron Stein, Eddie Donno, Greg Barnett, Jeff Imada, Nick Brandon, Kiante Elam, Jon Epstein, Rick LeFevour, Harry Wowchuk, Nick Gillard, Chuck Jeffreys, Charlie Picerni, Jeff Cadiente, Jery Hewit, Calvin Brown, Vince Capone, David Rowden, Cort Hessler, Manny Siverio, Charlie Picerni, Tim Gilbert, Steve and David Pope, Hiro Koda, Scott Dale, Robert Alonzo, Jill Brown, Al Jones, Kevin Scott, Mike Justice, Joey Box, Gary Powell and Mary Albee.

Special appreciation

Posthumously, I'd like to thank Bill from Bill's Stunt Service. Bill always made me feel right at home whenever I came to his office for a map to find the production location. A favorite saying of Bill's was "Hiya, Kiddo."

Special Salutes

I would like to thank my friend, confidant, prayer partner and editor, Michael Andre Adams, for without his patience and skillful editing this book would not be the same.

Owen of Bill's Stunt service: Thanks for hooking a sista up!

Joni's Stunt Service: For never giving up until you found me!

Missy of Missy's Stunt Service: when you were looking for me. Thank you for all the great jobs you referred and for Jared's great voice.

Michelle Braverman, my agent at Action Aces (KSR Agency): Thank you for always keeping it REAL Heidi Hydar of Action Aces (KSR Agency): Thank you for the extra spice

Kendal Park, at JLA Agency: Thank you for your understanding when I was doing my STUNTS

My Manager, Sharyn Berg: For your understanding, guidance and believing in me.

Helene Sokol: My manager when I first came to Los Angeles.

Peter Bucossi: For continuously calling me for NY Under Cover

April Weeden Washington: For diligently recommending me when I first came to Los Angeles

Buddy Love and Mike Lee: For the "Angela Davis kicking it like Avis " solid laughs

Jay Lynch, Norb Phillips, Debbie Evan and Sean Graham: For being such great mentors

Kym Washington: For the long talks and listening sessions early on in my career

The ladies of V10

Lafaye Baker and the "Diamond in the Raw Awards"

Jennifer Webster and "The World Taurus Stunt Awards"

Karate Teachers Master Giacobe, Master Ricks, Master Walker, Master Wright and Marcus Salgado

Eric Betts: My fight and reaction trainer

Rick and Lori Seaman and the Motion Picture Driving Clinic crew: For teaching me the secret of the Juice- E- Lift

****

And, finally, I thank my family:

To my mom, for being my biggest cheerleader and taping every show, movie or commercial that she was able to catch on television.

To my brother-turned-sniper who, along with all of his friends and their rough housing, helped to prepare me for a career in the stunt business. He continues to tease me about my career performing stunts for the camera while he's out keeping the streets safe.

To my sisters for understanding why I missed so many trips, parties and other family events.

To the rest of my family and dear friends for your love, support and encouragement that continues to cheer me on.

To the man in my life: For all of your love, support and constant reminders that I am "a bad mutha ... shut ya mouth!"

To my daughter, who inspires me and pushes me to be a better person. Mommy loves you.

Made in the USA
Las Vegas, NV
17 January 2022

41635019R00092